CONCILIUM   2000/3

RELIGION DURING AND AFTER COMMUNISM

Edited by

Miklós Tomka and Paul M. Zulehner

SCM Press · London

Published by SCM Press, 9–17 St Albans Place,
London N1

Copyright © Stichting Concilium

English translations © 2000 SCM–Canterbury Press Ltd

ISBN: 0 334 03059 5

Typeset by Regent Typesetting, London
Printed by Biddles, Ltd, Guildford and King's Lynn

Concilium Published February, April, June, October,
December.

Contents

Introduction: Religion During and After Communism –
In Eastern Central Europe
MIKLÓS TOMKA and PAUL M. ZULEHNER   5

Resistance: Testimony and Encapsulation
JAN SOKOL   12

Underground Church: Participation of the Laity or Sectarianism?
OTO MÁDR   20

A Theology of the Second World? Observations and Challenges
ANDRÁS MÁTÉ-TÓTH   27

A Rise in Atheism
ALBERT FRANZ   36

Social Upheaval and the Phenomenon of Atheism: Two Challenges
MILOSLAV CARDINAL VLK   44

Pastoral Work and the Shock of Modernization
JANUSZ MARIANSKI   52

The Marginalization of Christians in Eastern Central Europe
MIKLÓS TOMKA   62

The Change in the Religious Situation in the Eyes of Non-Believers
MARKO KERŠEVAN   74

Modes of Religious Education in Slovenia
STANKO GERJOLJ   82

Priests and Religious Orders
VINKO POTOCNIK   89

Religion and Media
LÁSZLÓ LUKÁCS   97

Still Building Bridges: Eastern Europe's Church in the World Church
JONATHAN LUXMOORE   106

Encounters Between East and West in the Renewal of Pastoral Work
PAUL M. ZULEHNER   115

Contributors   123

Introduction: Religion During and After Communism – In Eastern Central Europe

MIKLÓS TOMKA AND PAUL M. ZULEHNER

Eastern Central Europe looks back on traumatic events. First it became one of the main theatres of the Second World War. Then in Teheran (1943) and Yalta (1945) it was sold off, like Joseph by his brothers (Gen. 37.28) – by France, Great Britain and the United States. Eastern Central Europe was handed over to the Soviet Union. For half a century it had to live under foreign rule; the Communism which was forced on it exercised a rule of violence against individuals, tradition and people. In particular Communism wanted to destroy religion and the church. The Marxist ideology regarded these as the embodiment of evil, and in practical politics as the most significant opponents of totalitarianism.

So the Christians came under pressure. The church lost institutions and possessions. In most countries of the region the Catholic Church of the Eastern Rite (the Greek Catholic Church) was banned or declared part of Orthodoxy; with a few exceptions the religious orders were also banned. The church schools, the social institutions, the Christian organizations and the media suffered the same fate. Even religious practices were penalized; organized Christian education of the youth and the formation of religious base-groups and small communities were actually judged 'conspiracy against the state' and condemned. So the Christians of Eastern Central Europe paid a high price in blood for their convictions, and for decades were systematically discriminated against. The number of martyrs – in the strictest sense of the word – and the extent to which the faithful were disadvantaged have made the last half-century a special era in church history.

The Party state was first conceived of in accordance with ideological notions, but in time it developed into the rule of a party bureaucracy.[1] At all events, the Communist autocracy sought to model society by its own judgment, or even for its own benefit. The will of ordinary people, tradition or majority votes had no say here. Whole peoples became guinea-pigs. As objects of vivisection the church and Christians had to safeguard their survival and testify to their Lord. This gave Christianity in the Communist era a special character. Jan Sokol provides a vivid description of the pressures on Christians and the difficulties that they experienced.

What alternatives were there? The two extreme positions were, on the one hand identifying with the system and becoming dogsbodies for it, and on the other retreating from the world. The first option is usually attributed to the 'peace priests'; among the laity such an attitude was bound up with leaving the church and losing faith. For priests there were three possible reasons for identifying with the system. Very few of them put themselves at the disposal of the state for their own benefit. And there were only a few so blinded that they regarded socialism as it really existed as the best possible form of society in the given circumstances. Those who acted in this way out of conviction were rewarded by the state with advantages and favours – also and not least for their church. Sokol puts the famous Reformed theologian Josef Hromadka in this category for the period before 1968. Presumably the Hungarian primate of the 1970s and 1980s, Cardinal Lékai, would belong in the same group. However, the most frequent reason for this 'priesthood of peace' was that many could have been broken by torture and imprisonment or compelled to yield with the threat of exposing secret sins. This last group suffered from their own weaknesses all their lives.

The opposite pole, retreat from the world, could have been the result of a sober assessment of the situation. Some thought that the church could survive Communism only by hibernating underground. Another pattern was more frequent. Men and women supported Christianity and its dissemination in ordinary life and as a result were regarded by the police as criminals. Once they had been noticed, their legal possibilities were extremely limited. So often the only way was into the underground. Oto Mádr gives two accounts of this, relating to local conditions.

Some groups could be put under observation by the organs of state down to the last member. In the constant bombardment which followed they had nothing to lose. They attempted to set limits to their persecution by appeals to the public. Such exemplary witnesses were occasionally idealized by Western observers, who could get only a very inadequate view of the situation, as the only true confessors. Here the danger of sectarianism was easily forgotten. Mádr speaks of the 'prophetic consciousness' but also of 'special behaviour'. In addition there was the fact that people set themselves above the norms of theology and church law and – in the Hungarian case discussed – in principle rejected a leadership in the church which had not been chosen from below. The elitist consciousness which regarded as lax all those who could avoid political confrontation could also be divisive. Here Hungary's P.Bulányi and his movement alienated themselves not only from the bishops but also from the majority of other Christians and movements. Finally, the tendency towards fundamentalism made the group mentioned politically predictable. The state could use the dispute between brothers and sisters for purposes of manipulation.

By contrast, the everyday life of Christians in Eastern Central Europe ran between these two extreme positions. It consisted in the search for responsible compromises, in balancing Christian testimony and participation in the life of a Communist state. The more exposed the position that someone occupied, the more delicate the attempt became. Opportunities differed from country to country. Conditions varied depending on whether the church remained a great power and knew that the whole people was behind it (as in Poland), or whether it could gain sympathies only from the underground (as in Czechia); they were different yet again where a relatively broad field of church activity remained open, but the bishops were chosen by the state and the priests had to suffer the most stringent state control of their activity (as in Hungary). Among the co-ordinates in question was defining the point at which one had to say no, even if this disrupted one's own existence or interrupted the pastoral care of thousands. But it would have been irresponsible not to engage in the struggle simply because one repudiated Communism in principle. It was comparatively simple to avoid the cross of the situation and the doubts of compromise by simply giving way or even ghettoizing oneself in intransigent opposition. The great majority of believers managed to keep going as Christians. Of course, here too people could put their heads in the sand. But to join in the struggle was more responsible than to escape into one or other extreme position.

The political change of 1989/90 represented a fundamental upheaval: life took completely new courses. The significance of the immediate past for the future became just as questionable as whether the countries of the former Eastern block belonged together. There were no plans for this X Day. To begin with, the time called for improvisations, but these did not replace reflection. This was how the search for determinative force of the past first began. Andras Máté-Tóth reflects on a genuinely Eastern Central European theology. For the most part this is still a thing of the future, but it is indispensable if the countries of this region are not uselessly to squander their specific experiences.

An important characteristic of some former Communist countries (these include above all the former DDR, i.e. the new federal Länder of Germany, and the Czech Republic) is the wide spread of atheism. This is really not a post-Christian condition, but one untouched by Christianity. Quite a few countries have been able to erect a real barrier between the religious and the religionless part of the population. The delays in social communication and the exclusion of religion from public life have helped to make this barrier impenetrable. Now the parties are meeting; the opening-up of an un-hindered public life is providing surprises. But atheism is certainly not a Communist or even an East European characteristic. Thus the change in political conditions has not automatically altered it. On the contrary, the unification of Europe is leading to new alloys. Albert Franz analyses the challenges which this presents to theology and the church and which point beyond Eastern Central Europe.

The change has brought freedom and thus a new responsibility in action. As under Communism, the differences between the countries continue to be immense. Some countries must begin right from the bottom. One example of this is the Czech Republic, as is shown by the article by Cardinal Vlk, the President of the Council of European Bishops' Conferences (CCEE). In another context he illustrates the Czech situation like this: 'in one deanery of the Archdiocese of Prague with 26 parishes from the pre-Communist period there are only 5 priests. 8,780 faithful live scattered over them, of whom 492 are practising Catholics. Granted, that is an extreme example, but it is significant. That means that on average a parish has about 300 faithful, of whom 20 practise.'[2] That is clearly a missionary situation.

Another problem area is the unbroken and strong Christian tradition which is now coming up against modernity. For several authors the shock of modernization is a key concept. Must we expect a helpless assimilation? Or can the general, living traditional piety counter secularization? Janusz Marianski deals with Poland, but similar considerations are also relevant to Slovakia, Croatia and Romania. The real question is how strongly the autonomy of social-cultural change must be estimated to be. Can it be overcome? Each country has to find its own answer. To overestimate the determinative force of social and economic pressure would be as devastating as to overestimate one's own capacities.

In general it may be said that Christians in Eastern Central Europe find themselves in a comparatively disadvantageous social situation. Though the reason for this now may be their numerical weakness or a delay in development, at all events the Christians and the churches of Eastern Central Europe cannot rely on their own social weight (with the possible exception of Poland). In that case, what options remain open? Miklós Tomka writes about this. At all events the chief need is really to perceive the situation and to reject any nostalgia.

The background against which the new life is beginning has been staged by Communism. The past cannot be undone: it lives on not least in the elites and in the way in which non-Christians think. The debate here is not over the question who is right and to what degree. It is enough to note that in the new democracies different people live side by side with different views. But a democratic disposition, subsidiarity and a pluralistic civil society are by no means universally affirmed. There are conflicts of interest. The recognition of the rights of the church and the restitution of its former property may have a good basis in law and be unavoidable. Nevertheless this can lead to tensions and hinder the fulfilment of the church's mission. It is not easy to decide where the church is to establish its rights and where it is to forego legitimate demands in favour of its mission. Marko Krševan sketches a perspective in which non-Christians can see the change in position of the church and its behaviour after Communism. No church in Eastern Central Europe can live up to its task if it has not taken such views seriously. A dialogue with the non-believing part of society and even that part which is hostile to the church is one of the most urgent tasks of the churches.[3]

There are also concrete questions which must be resolved quickly in Eastern Central Europe. Communism gravely curtailed the possibilities of religious education and practised a materialistic indoctrination in all public institutions. Today socialists and liberals call these same institutions and courses 'ideologically neutral' and will not understand the desire of Christians for their own education. There is no accepted answer to the question whether Christians should advocate their conviction in public institutions or whether the church needs its own educational institutions to strengthen the Christian identity of believers. The answer is connected both with the strength of religion in a particular country and also the degree to which the public atmosphere is hostile to religion. Stanko Gerjolj offers reflections from a Slovenian perspective, i.e. from the perspective of a country which is predominantly Catholic but also massively secularized, in which the persecution of religion was more reasonable than in most other former Communist countries.

The question of the priesthood also shows the plurality of Eastern Central

Europe. Vinko Potocnik gives a survey. With the exception of Poland, Communism also damaged the training of priests everywhere. Since the change, a rise in vocations can be noted (again Poland is the exception, but now in the opposite direction). The numbers and the social expectations give grounds for optimism. However, priests in Eastern Central Europe face tasks for which they are hardly prepared. They have to find a new way of being the church. They have to contribute to the development of active and mature lay people and also to the public role and public testimony of the church.

The relationship to the secular world is generally an area which causes the church difficulties. Neither the pre-Communist practice of interweaving the state with a church which at that time was powerful nor the ghettoized situation or underground existence of past decades can provide useful starting points. László Lukács' article helps to survey the scene in the church media: he traces the notable build-up in this sphere. The difficulties clearly lie less at a technological and organizational level than in fear of the world and the undeveloped capacity for communication. To overcome this is one of the most important tasks of the churches of Eastern Central Europe.

Last but not least, it should not be forgotten that Eastern Central Europe is part of Europe and that the churches of these countries are parts of the world church. Those are historical and geographical realities. But Communism has dug deep ditches. Jonathan Luxmoore describes how the building of bridges appears to someone with knowledge of Poland who looks with Western eyes. Potocnik had already pointed out that half of the Christians of Europe live in Eastern or Eastern Central Europe. That also creates new conditions in the church with the fall of the walls. It is equally important for both East and West to note this.

The Pastoral Forum in Vienna is one bridge-building firm. It attempts to encourage the independence of the Christians and churches of Eastern Central Europe and to enable them to act. Paul M.Zulehner sketches out the priorities and puts these efforts in the framework of pastoral theology. This includes further education and the creation of basic information. Over the past four or five years the analysis of the situation has been advanced in ten countries with the 'New Departures' project. Teams for reflection have been established in each of these countries. They consist not only of social scientists but also of clergy and Christians who are intended to guarantee the infiltration of the insights gained into the church. The present issue of *Concilium* must also be regarded as a fruit of this long undertaking.[4] However, the real fruits must mature locally. It can only be hoped that the bridge-builders will multiply and that the churches will finally take courage and cross the bridges.

Translated by John Bowden

Notes

1. Milovan Djilas, *The New Class*, New York 1957; Michael S.Voslesensky, *Nomenklatura*, Vienna, Munich, Zurich and Innsbruck 1980.
2. Miloslav Cardinal Vlk, 'Kirche in Osteuropa: herrschen oder dienen?', in Wolfgang Grycz (ed.), *Kirche in Osteuropa: herrschen oder dienen? 1. Internationaler Kongress Renovabis 1997*, Friesing nd, 46–60: 53.
3. See the Pastoral Constitution of the Second Vatican Council, 'The Church in the Modern World', no.76, on the relationship between the political community and the church.
4. The journal *Concilium* is especially grateful to Paul M.Zulehner for giving time and effort towards devising and producing this issue.

Resistance: Testimony and Encapsulation

JAN SOKOL

Experience can be communicated only to a very limited degree. Those who have lived under Communism lack the necessary detachment, and those who have not can only have the palest of ideas. Moreover in Eastern Europe 'Communism' was a whole era, with very different phases, and different in each of the countries, depending on the initial conditions and the social and social-psychological presuppositions. So even someone who has lived intensively under Communism for more than forty years can at best attempt a case study from his own perspective: a reflective recollection and by no means a sociologically relevant survey.

1. The legacy of the 1950s

Although my country, Czechia, suffered substantially less in the war than e.g. Poland, for us the liberation by the Soviet Army was a real liberation with far-reaching effects. A strong left-wing and partly also Communist movement in the pre-war period with important intellectuals; the debacle of 1938/1939 interpreted as betrayal by our Western allies; hundreds of thousand of victims and the unbelievable terror of the concentration camps related by those who survived – that was a framework of the short interim period of more or less freedom which lasted until 1948. The wind blew to the left, as it also did in the West at the time. Thus Stalin was so certain of his future success in what was then Czechoslovakia that as early as 1946, when the Western armies withdrew in West Bohemia, he withdrew the Red Army. No Russian troops were stationed here between 1946 and 1968.

Fascistic movements were quite insignificant in the pre-war period and open collaboration with the Nazis was rare. The poor 'President' of the Protectorate was a pious Catholic, and despite numerous clergy who became the victims of concentration camps there was no widespread persecution of the church. The Nazis shamelessly misused the saintly Wenzel for propaganda purposes, and this rebounded on the Catholic Church after the end of the war. Moreover at that time the church still had very clear traces of the era of the Austrian empire about it and was generally dependent on the peasant tradition, for which Sunday worship was a high point of social life: something that was taken for granted and not thought about. Granted, there was an intellectual Catholic renewal, but compared with the country masses it was very weak, and therefore also secondary in the eyes of pastors and bishops.

Soon after the Communists seized power in February 1948 the first trials began, and the dark time of real and deliberate persecution. The first victims were the intellectuals, then the members of the religious orders: in 1950 all the religious houses were dissolved and all monks and bishops interned. The attempt to found a 'national' Catholic movement against Rome under the leadership of some collaborating priests failed surprisingly quickly – thus especially the Catholics became suspect second-class citizens. Significantly Bishop Tochta of Litomiče, who attempted for the longest time to negotiate with the powers, was the first to be imprisoned. Hundreds of priests, active laity, pathfinders, etc., followed him. This was the road to extermination.

The situation with the Protestant minority was rather different. The leading theologian Josef Hromadka, who was a really significant figure and who had spent the war in the USA, shared the conviction of many intellectuals that socialism was a historically necessary development which the church had not to resist and, despite certain objections, in the end he took Stalin's Communism seriously. Although he is in no way to be included among the collaborators, he did perform valuable service to the Communist powers (e.g. in the peace movement) and in part gave them international legitimation, but on the other hand he did negotiate substantially better conditions for his church. Under his leadership many Protestants became honourable Communists and some of them only painfully saw through the system after 1968 – again together with him. The destruction of the peasant class by so-called collectivization was very brutal: a co-operative had to be formed in each village, often under the leadership of landless people (postmen, craftsmen, etc.), and anyone who refused to join was put behind bars. Some staged violent incidents, followed by many death sentences, were meant to legitimate the harshness. More than 100,000 of these stubborn, resolute and loyal supporters of a peasant tradition spent long years in the camps and then returned as strangers to their now deeply changed villages – sometimes strangers even to their own changed families. Thus the Catholic Church came to be in a very oppressed situation. The church structures were destroyed and its spiritual centres obliterated. In the country the natural village authorities were now degraded to 'kulaks' and enemies of the state; the pastors were either in prison or under the thumb of the 'church secretaries' – and even in the city each had to seek his own way.

Most of what in 1948 was still an 80% Catholic majority have now given up any ties with the church – which often in any case were only formal, both in the country and among the middle classes. The defective religious education, so typical of traditional Catholicism, could offer no resistance to these circumstances. The rest, who were better prepared, were under constant pressure. Their first duty was now to remain faithful: to the church, to the imprisoned bishops, the pope and perhaps also Jesus Christ. Any religious activity outside the liturgy was dangerous, and those who even showed their faith openly felt the consequences. Not only leading positions but also many professions were now forbidden to a Christian, like that of teacher; children might not study, and those who sought spiritual reading often had to copy it out for themselves: this was how the first Samizdat came into being. But a notorious believer had to resist not only the quasi-official pressure but often also the incomprehension or mockery of his or her fellow believers; earlier Czech society had not been particularly 'religious' and was antipathetic towards the Catholic Church for historical reasons.

The course of the individual was now determined particularly by the family. Some sought compromises by making various concessions and paid for them with more or less hypocrisy, with carefully hidden and fleeting attendance at worship, often in a remote place, with various 'engagements' (as they were then called) in the trade unions, youth organizations or the 'unity' associations. Membership of the People's Party (which had been annexed) was also a protection if one was forced to join the Communist Party. Those to whom this way was already closed by the experience of their own families were best off among the workers. Even in the 1950s the air was essentially freer in a work place, and there honest, good people were often to be found among the (rare) Communists.

For the whole weight of those years – especially in Czechia – was not just stamped by state violence and its threats. As a result of its resistance to Hitler, the Communist Party at that time still had a certain authority, a significant intellectual potential and a host of convinced members, especially among the workers who experienced the wretchedness of the 1930s. And with such people it was also possible to speak freely in all honesty. Was what was happening now just a necessary price for a juster society, or was it conversely a farce which concealed quite base aims? But in a society without public opinion such quite serious discussions had to remain strictly private. The Czech Catholic Church and its faithful withstood the hard test of the

1950s well and produced thousands of unknown heroes. Its success when things began to loosen up was more problematical. The Party was still able quietly to suppress the first rumours within the Communist Party after Stalin's death, after Kruschchev's disclosures and after the upheavals in Poland and Hungary in 1956. However, towards the end of the 1950s the discontent of convinced Communists could no longer be held back: the economy was in difficulties and it was no longer possible to overlook the backward state of science and technology. Thus one could often find that at work loud criticism could be heard of a session of the Communist Party. The dividing wall between the party members (up to 1.5 million of them) and the rest of us 'reactionaries' (as we were then called) continued to exist, but despite certain setbacks individual contacts had become more numerous and more open.

In the course of the 1950s the democratic and the Christian opposition could be shattered in so far as the development of the 1960s was mainly supported by the Party, or its enlightened members. The air had become freer in the cultural sphere and in science – though with many compromises – and the first prisoners also came back. Some were embittered, even defeated, but many were also simply glad to have survived, some even as victors. The first holes appeared in the harsh and simple black-and-white world of the 1950s – and the faithful suddenly faced new questions. Their church continued to be in a state of siege, without bishops and without religious houses, strictly limited to liturgy. But in other respects the dangers and threats had diminished, and slowly new possibilities opened up in the secular world, first of all in culture. Are the concessions required tolerable? What is still worth doing? How far can one go without losing oneself?

When one of the most gifted theologians, Josef Zverina, was released after many years, he spread a radiant optimism around him. After six months he confided to me in a conversation how much more complicated he found life in freedom, limited though it was: 'In prison any decision was easier: in any case it was completely clear what was wrong and what was right.' Another time, when the question was about a publication in the 'Catholic' press – directed by a quite evil 'peace priest' – he reflected and then said with a smile: 'You're younger. You can speak with him – I can't.'

2. Movement in the 1960s

During the 1960s the frontiers of the state also opened up – hesitantly – first only towards the East. Thus in 1961 for the first time I looked with wonder at the church in the then DDR, its great men and its possibilities. And at the same time came the first visits from the West: brave and wise people, who cautiously sought to make contacts and brought the books that we ardently desired. For those of us who had had enough of the strict encapsulation of the 1950s, that was a provocative time. What, how and where next? We found the first occasion for public activity as Christians with the Protestants. Since 1962 the ecumenical world had been the first place in which Christians could meet as Christians and talk freely about religious questions. Soon after that there also came the first translations of new theology, with the figure of Teilhard de Chardin towering over all, and the Council and its enthusiasm: a new world opened up. But with the thaw also came the first disillusionments. When Archbishop Beran of Prague, a former concentration camp victim, was allowed to go to Rome after twenty years of internment and Tomasek took his place, the pope appeased some of the worst collaborators and 'peace priests' with high honours, whereas even in the best cases the true heroes had to wait another twenty years. When this development then culminated in spring 1968 it could already be seen clearly how different the standpoints of the Catholics now were – stamped by the bitter experiences which only an authentic faith can get over. A Czech proverb says that one can even get used to the gallows. In fact, under the pressure and the fear of the 1950s people had developed effective defence mechanisms which in the course of time could even be comfortable. Sunday worship – completely inconspicuous. The family or just a couple of friends. Anything else is alien and suspicious to me. I do what I'm told – more cannot be expected of me. The 1968 spring in fact began as a movement within the Communist Party, accompanied by bold criticism from the intellectuals and students. But then when real possibilities opened up, most Catholics held back in a cautious wait-and-see attitude. Thus 1968 remained predominantly an urban, even a Prague concern. And then in August, when the Russians came, some felt this to be confirmation of this cheap cunning. Nevertheless then at least a Catholic generation had to live spiritually by what had appeared around 1968.

However, in May 1968, on the initiative of some released Catholic prisoners, an open letter was published which supported the development and generously offered forgiveness and reconciliation. The first gathering of the newly founded 'Work of Conciliar Renewal' in Velehrad was a great festival with many thousand participants and a promising programme. What originally began as a lay initiative of a Prague psychologist by the name of Nemec and was then also supported by the bishops, seemed to be pioneering an opening-up of Catholicism, but unfortunately only for a very short time.

I hope that my view of the time after 1968 is not just governed by my own age. It soon became bitter disappointment. It was the very leaders of 1968 who step by step disowned the whole thing. Bravery, readiness, solidarity – for what? Woe to anyone who was concerned with more than his own family: 'Any good deed will unexpectedly be punished as it deserves' was and still is the saying. The disappointed hopes and the deep humiliation, the gentle yet effective pressure towards self-surrender, bound up with the social blood-letting of 200,000 refugees, produced a universal hangover, to which most Czechs, as always, responded with cynicism. No great victims and no great heroes: that is the message of Jan Palach (1969). The pastors who had hardly noticed the brief spring returned to their grey everyday life and now mostly devoted themselves to their church roofs. Thanks to them for that, too – some saved their lives this way.

The special characteristics of the 1970s and 1980s are on the one hand a black hopelessness. In the 1950s a great many people had expected in all earnest that in the autumn 'it' would 'crash'. They even laid bets on it. One of the very popular stories of the time spoke of the 'orange gas' with which the Americans would one day spray the whole of Central Europe and then occupy it without violence while it slept. Now all that was over. Communism seemed more stable than ever before, and that meant for ever. There were different reasons for this disarming tendency: the détente, the doctrine of 'peaceful co-existence' and so on were after all for the most part an expression of inner slackness, discouragement and cowardice. Under the gentler pressure the Catholics too not longer felt so firm, and so to speak were more and more accomplices in the universal caterwauling. Moreover most people saw the dissident movement as something more disturbing and alienating. Although the first idea of Charta 77 came from the Catholic Nemec, for the most part it was supported by former Communists.

But on the other hand the Party itself had changed. The convinced Communists of former times had partly now themselves become enemies of the state, and some of them went into exile: granted, not into the uranium mines but as night watchmen or window cleaners. There was no longer an 'armed fist of the working class' – how ridiculous that now sounded! – but a pragmatic and increasingly corrupt power organization which to some degree guided the headless and thoughtless state. One would seek Communists in vain there: a very radical friend who went to Holland in 1968 returned soon afterwards saying that here (as a street-sweeper) at least he would not meet any Communists. At any rate being a Christian and a Catholic was still a burden and in certain spheres a hindrance, but arrests remained rare and punishments in single figures. But that meant that the usual encapsulation lost all meaning; slowly it became more a matter of convenience. On the other hand now too the Party was no longer a real 'ideological' enemy; merely an access to a career.

3. The end of an era?

But after the 1960s something also changed quite imperceptibly in the inner attitude of Czech society to religion. The ridiculous side, the charge of obscurantism, disappeared, and as early as 1968 a large part of the Czech intelligentsia in all seriousness expected a great deal from the church and especially from the Catholic Church. In part this opportunity was already missed at that time, which later could be excused by the brevity of the 'starting window'.

In the second half of the 1980s, unprejudiced people were already clear how much Communism had now been evacuated. The rumours about Polish Solidarity and about Russian Perestroika aroused new hopes and instilled rather more courage in many people. The first sign was the great pilgrimage at Velehrad (1985) with 150,000 participants, where the surprised Party speakers were simply booed, this time not by Prague intellectuals but by the Catholic 'people'. There followed the petition for freedom of religion with half a million signatures and at the same time, on the eve of the change, the solemn beatification of St Agnes (11 November 1989), which was even broadcast by state television. One special story is the personal development of Cardinal Archbishop Tomasek of Prague. When he came to Prague in 1965 he was a loveable but almost anxious man who only over the years – under the influence of Zverina and then especially of Pope Wojtyla – became the charismatic leader not just of the Catholic Church. His public appearances in November 1989 contributed greatly to the success of the change and brought the Catholic Church to the pinnacle of friendly expectations in public opinion.

Finally a few words about the further development. Since 1990 the churches have enjoyed complete freedom – that is the first and most important thing. However, the Catholic Church in particular feels the painful lack of at least a generation of educated and open priests and theologians. All the bishops' sees are occupied, with the best men available. The religious houses have been restored, but most of them lack new members.

The Prague theological faculty, now again part of the university, has skilfully outmanoeuvred all the new teachers and maintained its encapsulation. The church government allowed itself to be drawn into the hopeless and senseless fight over the restoration of property. The old stereotype revived and did great damage to the church's reputation. For the most part the Catholic Church as a whole is still supported by the traditional country population, which perhaps makes up three-quarters of the practising faithful. This orientation – of course, seen from within – makes it incomprehensible to the urban and educated population. The church presents itself as a closed community representing the interests of people of a particular kind who have little to offer to others. Thus the largely lively interest of young people with their questions and hopes also turns in another direction, to the sects and even more towards a 'free', i.e. uncommitted 'religiosity' which does not cost anything. This mission field is hard to reach, but it promises much. Who can convincingly offer the message of Jesus to these people – and bear witness?

Translated by John Bowden

Underground Church: Participation of the Laity or Sectarianism?

OTO MÁDR

In the twentieth century the peoples of Eastern Central Europe had to fight twice for their existence on both the political and the spiritual level. The churches above all were in a bad situation because the official structures of leadership had been narrowed down, paralysed or made completely power-less. Under alien Soviet rule the situation of the Catholic Church differed in the various countries. Any political-ideological activity was strictly for-bidden everywhere. The strictly church life of the East Germans, Poles, Slovenes and Croats remained more or less free, whereas there were many restrictions for Hungary and Czechoslovakia. The Czechoslovak Communist Party set itself the goal of making Czechoslovakia the first atheist state in the world after Albania.

I. Group 1: the less threatened churches

In the DDR the bishops could, for example, forbid Catholics to join the socialist youth movement; they could train lay staff for their kindergartens and hospitals in their own schools. In Poland not only the many bishops but also educated laity could discuss public concerns, for example in their press. The Catholic university lived on, though with restrictions; a mass of seminaries trained many priests. In Yugoslavia only 'religious propaganda' was forbidden in public; otherwise the life of the church remained free. In 1970 diplomatic relations between Yugoslavia and the Holy See were even restored.

In Slovenia 'the Catholic Church was able to maintain its presence and spiritual authority thanks to loyalty to itself and thanks to its unity with the pastors'.[1] Everywhere it was the loyalty of the church people, i.e. the laity, which decided how Christian faith and its servant, the official church, would survive. In the countries of the second group, church life was far more diffi-cult, also for laity, and their role in particular was very important.

II. Group 2: the threatened churches

1. Czechoslovakia

In the state of this name from 1918 to 1939 and from 1945 to 1992 two nations very close in language but culturally different coexisted: the more secularized Czechs and the strongly traditional Slovaks. However, an extraordinary impulse came from this smallest of the neighbouring peoples for the two others. As early as 1943, i.e. before the Soviet occupation, the Croatian ex-Jesuit Tomislav Kolakovic fled from the Germans to the Slovak capital of Bratislava with the intention of preparing in Eastern Central Europe a spiritual defence against the threat of a violent de-Christianization and a mission from Russia. There he won over convinced Catholics for this broad vision, especially students, and with them formed the central activist group 'Family'. This began with the organization of the Catholic underground movement on the model of Joseph Cardijn's Belgian *Jeunesse ouvrière chrétienne* (CAJ). Kolakovic provided the leaders of the various groups with the necessary spiritual, but also theological, philosophical and sociological equipment in exercises and in courses.

Immediately after the end of the war two college students brought 'Family' to Prague and Czechia, where they could reinforce the beginnings of the underground CAJ and enlarge its methods and organization. The role of the laity was particularly important. For the very large student movement we priests prepared almost only written material for individual study. This movement spread spontaneously throughout the colleges. Several of their activists were then convicted of 'political crimes' in a series of trials and continued their apostolic mission in prisons.

Not only many priests and men and women religious but also individual faithful and their spontaneous groups fostered the freer underground life of the church. Catholic families were particularly loyal and important because of their influence on outsiders. For example the Kaplan family in Prague with its ten children also brought together young people and among other things cultivated Taizé spirituality. Lay catechists taught children 'illegal' catechesis in private homes.[2] After the 'Prague Spring' (1968) the organized Focolare movement could also spread itself quietly. Though without state apoproval, it was tolerated, probably also because in principle it was directed by laity. By comparison the police kept an eye on the secret Catholic literature (Samisdat) which grew rapidly and also punished it through the courts. The generous activity of laity was also decisive for the Samisdat.

The most striking underground movement, 'Koinotes', became known

abroad after the change in 1989.[3] The reason for this was the personality
of its founder Felix Davidek, with bold plans for reform which he realized
himself. I got to know him well over the course of several years that we spent
in prison together. He was extraordinary gifted and fluent, with a tendency
towards being a poly-historian, but relatively little interested in the study of
theology. As a young priest he had the dream of founding and directing a
Catholic university.

After the Communist purging of the colleges in 1947 he organized secret
substitute study for the students who had been expelled. After a failed
attempt to escape abroad he spent 1952–1954 in prison. There he had a new
idea: the Communist power will last a long time and liquidate all bishops and
priests. Therefore it is necessary to build up a secret hierarchy and a secret
clergy. He managed to attach himself to the line of secret bishops established
by Rome and in being consecrated bishop.

Immediately after that he began to build up what was in practice an
autonomous underground church. Contrary to the Roman prohibitions,
repeated after 1970, he consecrated sixteen bishops, and some of these
consecrated a further nine. The number of priests ordained in the underground was far greater. This secret reserve was to be appointed only when
the regular hierarchy had been exterminated. Contrary to this gloomy
prognosis, however, the political situation improved. Catholic laity put
increasingly strong public pressure on the government. The Minister of
Culture had to suffer loud protests at the great pilgrimage in Velehrad in
1985; in 1988 the petition composed by some lay people with a demand for
human freedoms for believers and all others was signed by more than half a
million people.

Meanwhile Davidek developed an original doctrine, theological and
mixed with other elements. He abandoned his previous predilection for
Thomism and found new inspiration in Pierre Teilhard de Chardin. He
stated that it was the prime duty of Christians to hasten the evolution of the
world to Point Omega – the return of Jesus Christ. He made an effort also to
carry this vision on a mission to other countries, e.g. Slovakia and the Soviet
Union, Hungary and Romania.

With this prophetic self-confidence he felt legitimated to go beyond the
limits of church law. Thus he consecrated married men not only priests but
also bishops. Formally he did that for the Greek Catholic Church, though its
canon law does not recognize married bishops. Furthermore he summoned
his bishops and other members of Koinotes (a third of the laity) to a 'synod'
to vote on the ordination of women to the priesthood. Certainly there was

serious resistance, and the vote ended indecisively. Nevertheless, the very next day Davidek ordained administered priestly ordination to his secretary, who later became his vicar-general.[4] Later he also ordained other women. For this reason individuals or groups left Koinotes, as others had already done for other reasons. Felix Davidek died in 1988.

After the change in 1989, all the priests who had been ordained secretly were offered the possibility of engaging in public pastoral work in the dioceses. Many who were unmarried accepted, and after a short examination and further training they went to parishes. By analogy, married priests could enter the service of the Greek Catholic Church or take on a task as deacons. Doubts as to whether all the ordinations performed by Davidek were valid caused a problem. The reason for this doubt lay in the fact that sometimes Davidek acted very strangely. Therefore new conditional ordinations were required by Rome. Only a hard core rejected them and stylized themselves in the role of a church of the future.[5] In the polarized Czech church of today, Davidek serves as a support for the progressives, though his project ended in a more clerical way.

In Slovakia some of Davidek's bishops disseminated his Koinotes movement, which was disapproved of by the underground church. By contrast, the movement founded by Kolakovic continued its activities without any appearance of being a sect. It lives on under the name Fatima.

2. Hungary

The first impulse towards the strongest underground movement of Catholic laity in Hungary was a meeting between the Piarist father György Bulányi and Tomislav Kolkovic, who wanted to prepare the church of Central Europe for Soviet occupation. In the year 1945, in Debrecen he founded four secret groups of activists. He handed over one of them to the young Piarist with the directive that he should educate the young people in such a way that they could live independent lives as Christians and engage in apostolic activities.

From these beginnings Bulányi developed a movement of small groups. They met with the desire of the Catholic elite with a spiritual orientation. The aim 'was to initiate a Catholicism with authentic qualities, which was to be based on the decisions of the individual. This called for a demanding spirituality, and its members were to be prepared to face the tribulations of "modern" life and Marxism for an appropriate apologetic on behalf of Christianity for the time'.[6] 'We began something quite new,' wrote Bulányi.

'We took the holy scriptures into our own hands . . . We discovered analogies between our groups living in the underground and the first Christians.'[7]

Here the world too was to be served, with a love embracing the whole world which was to offer a humanist alternative to the nationalist and anti-semitic mood of the time. This movement, fed by exercises and pamphlets – like other underground movements and small groups of the time – was interrupted by Stalinist measures, because among others even Bulányi was given prison sentences (1952–1956 and 1958–1960). After that, the movement began to revive to new life. From a group of priests, a group of older and a group of younger laity, a movement grew with thousands of members. The founder exercised his striking role of leadership, spiritually by practical recommendations and later also by his original theology. Despite his very powerful personality he called on the members to show the mentality of freethinking and dialogue.

This movement (in Hungary called Bokor or 'shrub') wanted to remain within the church and at its service. The first test of this attitude was the agreement made between the Communist state and the Catholic Church in 1964 within the framework of the then Vatican 'policy towards the East'. This weakened the inner tie between Bokor and the hierarchical church. The closer relationship which the new primate, Archbishop Lékai, entered into with the regime in 1976 had an even worse effect. Specifically, Bokor's internal opposition to collaboration with the state turned into an open dispute over the repudiation of military service. More serious, however, were Catholic objections to some theses from Bulányi's thought-world.

Bulányi is not a professional theologian but a pastor who thinks creatively. In the situation of persecution and especially of the failure of the church he discovered his prophetic mission, namely to prepare for a deep-seated renewal of the church and through it of the world. The guidelines for this have to be drawn directly from the gospel. But in addition there were also stimuli from some post-conciliar theologians and from reading *Concilium*.

Jesus himself, Bulányi argued, and not the magisterium or scholastic theology, must be regarded as the ultimate criterion. For this theology 'of Jesus' the actions of Jesus must be decisive, especially his concern for the suffering and the poor. He took over from Latin American theology the option for the poor as the nucleus of a true religion. Jesus did not save men and women by his vicarious death but through the example of his love, in service of love for humankind.

In practice this love is embodied in non-violence – and therefore a rejection of military service – and even in the eschatological extinction of the state, which is the main source of all violence. This is the reason for the sharp condemnation of the help of the church, if the life of believers is to be forced underground. The conscience trained in prayer and reading the Bible and controlled by conversations between brothers and sisters is set above any obedience. In this sense the underground church is to transform the whole church as leaven, and in this way the church is to influence the world.

Not all members of the movement could or wanted to put such claims into practice, so gradually many people went their own way. With the political liberation, the main reason for the base movement was also removed. It was only late in the 1990s that the Bulányi problem could be solved in the Hungarian church. Certain features of his thought led to a dispute with the bishops and in 1982 to the referral of his theses to Rome, where they were to be judged by the Congregation of Faith. Until this dispute was resolved, Bulányi was suspended, and publicly he could not exercise any priestly ministry.

For the Holy See the situation was a tricky one. People did not want either to condemn the bold freedom fighter or to damage the situation of the bishops in their negotiations with the state. The problem was resolved only in September 1997. Bulányi subscribed to twelve theses presented to him on the freedom of conscience;[8] in return the Hungarian Conference of Bishops repealed the prohibition on Bulányi's exercising priestly office.

Despite this success Bulányi does not feel fully accepted in today's Catholic Church; the change did not affect his life very much. With his theology and his activity as a writer after the change in 1990 he has (rightly?) opposed the rapid consolidation of the church situation. In this way he has marginalized himself; the movement has lost its 'ideological' basis. Some more recent initiatives of the movement, with which other Catholics and actions could co-operate, are successful examples of a contemporary pastoral practice which engages with modernity; here the authentic calls of Jesus can well serve as mediation. A closer and older group around Bulányi lives from the past and is no longer productive and inspiring; it makes up around 10% of the members (80–75 persons). Today the whole movement consists of around 700 persons, including the smallest in the large families. Many live their lives by Bulányi's moral traditions, without coming into structural contact with the rest of the movement.[9]

As well as Bokor, in Hungary there have been some short-lived attempts and three other organized underground movements which now live a public life without difficulties: Regnum Marianum, founded in 1900; Focolare; and the charismatic movement, which has been present in the country since the

1960s or 1970s. In addition there have been a spontaneous apostolate of the Christian life and many links among faithful believers.

Conclusion

The pressure of atheistic ideology has led not only to the heroism of a large number of believers but also to leaders with strong ideas and to some extreme phenomena. For all the differences, the approaches of Davidek and Bulányi have some things in common. Among other things, neither intended to disseminate their ideas outside the church but rather to implement them through reform of the church according to strict guidelines. That provides material enough for historians and theologians.

Translated by John Bowden

Notes

1. Ivan Viktor Papez, 'Lo stato giuridico dei fedeli in una comunità socialista', *Estudios juridico-canónicos* 141, Salamanca 1989, 85–97: 97.
2. There is a theological account of the church under threat by Oto Mádr, *Wie Kirche nicht stirbt. Zeugnis aus bedrängten Zeiten der tschechischen Kirche*, Leipzig 1993.
3. Monographs on Koinotes, *Ond ej Liska, Cirkev v podzemi a splolentsvi Koinotes* (The Underground Church and the Koinotes Fellowship), Brno 1999; Petr Fiala, Jiri Hanus, *Skryá církev. Felix Davidek a spoleenství Koinotes* (The Hidden Church. Felix M.Davidek and the Koinotes Community), Brno 1999.
4. Cf. the documentation in *Concilium* 1999/3 by Petr Fiala and Jirí Hanus, 126–38.
5. Jan Korec, 'La mia esperienza di vescovo clandestino', in *La Chiesa cattolica nell'Europea dell' Est. Persecutione, Libertà, Rinascità*, Königstein 1990, 22–8. Korec is one of the first three Jesuits to have been consecrated bishop with Rome's consent after February 1948.
6. András Maté-Tóth, *Bulányi und die Bokor Bewegung. Eine pastoraltheologische Würdigung*, Vienna 1992, 22. This Habilitation thesis by the long-term member of Bokor, accepted by the Vienna theological faculty, serves as the main source of this report.
7. Ibid., 23.
8. This addition relates to the Second Vatican Council Declaration on Religious Freedom (*Dignitatis humanae*).
9. A. Maté-Tóth, in a letter to O.Mádr of 8 January 2000.
10. Miklós Tomka, 'Wie das Lebenszeugnis der Gläubigen auf Ungläubige wirkt. Erfahrungen aus dem sozialistischen Land (Ungarn)', *Diakonia* 5, 1982, 329–33.

A Theology of the Second World?
Observations and Challenges

ANDRÁS MÁTÉ-TÓTH

The Reform countries of Eastern (Central) Europe[1] form a cultural region in the sense of Howard Odum's 'composite societal region'.[2] These countries are characterized above all by their community of destiny in the last fifty years, by the activities and techniques in forming a society which have developed in them, and by the characteristic nature of the ongoing development of their national and ethical traditions.

The collapse of the totalitarian regime in 1989 brought new political and economic structures, and confronted the societies of this cultural region with far-reaching challenges regarding their history, their national identity, their value structure and its future. The churches which, sometimes as pioneers, sometimes as fellow-travellers, sometimes as observers, have gone along with the origin of this new era, are called on by these developments to reflect again on their identity and their role in the new societies. The theology of these countries is challenged to note the cultural and social features of their world which are specific to the region and to reflect on them critically. In the following sections of this article I shall attempt to sketch out some points of this new reflection in church and theology. They form the contextual basis of a possible theology of (in) the Second World.

I. A land without milk and honey

Three fundamental points above all consist of problems related to the legacy of the Communist dictatorship in the Reform states: one is structural and political, one is anthropological and cultural, and one is ethical and moral.[3] Theologically these need to be analysed and commented on as signs of the time.

The *structural and political* shift represents a rapid transition: from a planned economy to the market economy including a process of privatization; from the one-party to the parliamentary multi-party system; from the total control of the public to the plurality of free expression of opinion; and to an extensive legal reform extending as far as the new legal regulation of international relations. This 'total' transformation of the societies activates existential anxieties and solutions (some of which are emotional and fundamentalist) brought up from the national past. Here a fissure can be observed between East and West. Western Europe is pragmatic, professional and orientated on the future – and therefore rationalistic, whereas among Eastern Europeans history, pathos, anger and a sense of injustice prevail. These characteristics and reflexes may no longer be fashionable at the end of the 1990s, but the anxiety about identity in these nations and societies stems from real historical experiences which Western Europeans have never experienced.[4]

From an *anthropological and cultural* perspective the 'spiritual cause' of the 'lack of orientation of so many people in the East' lies in the collapse of notions of progress characteristic of the Communist utopia. The 'pseudo-aestheticism and various kinds of pseudo-culture' of the DDR like uniforms, marches, flag ceremonies and rituals are also said to have left behind a real vacuum. Not least the fact that Marxism has thrown 'overboard the classic concept of person', which after all is the foundation of ethical knowing, has consequences. 'Up to 1985 in state-ordained atheism' the central concept of 'conscience remained unknown'. The social view of the time was focussed 'far too narrowly' only on productive work. The social status of individuals cannot be established by work alone. The dignity and value of human life has a greater significance. 'The forgotten realities about human beings' need to be recalled and new questions need to be asked about human anture.[5]

The *ethical and moral* devastation in the former socialist countries can be called a 'Chernobyl of souls'. People are no longer capable of professing any clear and permanent values and of making responsible decisions.[6] By comparison with West European modernity, here in the nineteenth and twentieth centuries an insignificant and inauthentic process of modernization has been taking place. The purpose-orientated and pragmatic actions or the values of the autonomy of the individual have not become as dominant as they are in Western Europe. The fact of subjection to a centralist power sealed this development. The great economic and political changes after the Second World War altered even traditional feelings and values of community from one moment to the next and opened up the way to a process which is called negative or empty modernization. This led to a reflex and meagre individualism which regardless of world-view, tradition or culture is concerned only for the accumulation of material values and survival.[7]

A large part of the population cherishes illusions which have developed since the collapse of the Communist dictatorship. Tensions and aggressiveness have grown in the Reform countries after the change. Nor has the new freedom by any means had only a positive effect on the church. The legacy of 'Sovietization' consists in passivity, a lack of initiative and an unwillingness to take responsibility. The church too needs 'help towards democratization' if it is to be able to fulfil its tasks.

II. Experiential basis

'It would be a delusion to think that the churches of Eastern Europe have emerged strengthened from oppression under the Communist regime' – thus Miloslav Vlk, Archbishop of Prague and President of the Council of European Bishops' Conferences (CCEE). The division into the 'East strong in the faith' and the 'godless West' of Europe which has often been propagated after the change is outmoded. But even now it is not yet easy to understand the ideological gulfs which have opened up through history. Some experts, bishops and theologians of the region observe that after all the Communist dictatorship also left marks on the churches which more or less offered resistance.[8]

1. Imprisonment

Biblical metaphors are often used to interpret and describe the history of persecution of the churches and Christians in this region. The total suppression of the church is emphasized with the image of the 'Egyptian captivity'. Under the Communist regimes the churches played the role of slaves: without rights, without means, on the threshold of the prisons or even going to the grave. In some countries the first epoch, that with a Stalinist stamp, lasted almost until the change (thus in the Ukraine and Romania); in other countries (in Poland, Hungary, Croatia and Slovenia) the harshness had already previously been declining steadily. The milder oppression opened up an increasing freedom for the churches, provided that they publicly confessed their loyalty to the goals of society – a church in the leading strings of the state. For this second period the image of the 'Babylonian captivity' is more appropriate, when the Jewish people enjoyed relative autonomy.

In the period of the dictatorship, above all practical and pastoral themes were at the centre of theological work. They were mostly disseminated in the circles of the so-called 'second public' – which was little, if at all, controlled by the state – as 'Samisdat'.[9] These works were hardly equipped with scholarly apparatus, but displayed a marked orientation on praxis and a high degree of creativity. They were often far removed from the specialist discussions of university theology and therefore closer to the problems of survival experienced by Christians in their immediate surroundings. The underground theologians almost all had a neo-scholastic training, but their works show an openness to an anthropological and contextual hermeneutics. The life and theological work of each underground theologian were deeply embedded in the catacomb world of the churches and as it were supported by it.[10]

Official theology, which was above all taught in the priests' seminars, had little intellectual freedom – varying in degree depending upon the country. In most countries for a long time it had to serve exclusively the new priests in training; in content and in teachers it was more controlled and separated from the world and often from the wandering people of God. In these circumstances it was a matter of course that at this level of theology works could be published which were theoretical and historical and 'context-less' in their social relevance.

2. *Anxieties about contact*

After the change, and in part already before it, those standpoints increased which sought an alternative between assimilation and resistance, traditionalism and renewal, between Vatican I and Vatican II, for churches and theology in the Second World also.

Tómás Halik, who until the beginning of 1993 was secretary of the Czech Conference of Bishops and since then has been professor at the Charles University in Prague, spoke out for openness. The emphasis of the Eastern European churches on their specific experience under Communism can appear to Western countries all too easily as a kind of martyr complex, which distorts rather than clarifies the pastoral challenges of the post-Communist period. Irritated and sometimes clearly on the defensive, by contrast the church of the countries of Central and Eastern Europe sees a threat from the West through secularism, consumerism and the profit-motive, and not least from the theology in the West, with which it had lost contact in the last decades of isolation. Often the churches of Eastern Europe regard theology as a 'luxury'. This position, according to Halik, harbours the danger of an 'easy pragmatism without reflection'. He calls for a theology which has grown out of experience under Communism, a 'theology after the gulag'.[11]

III. Theological traditions

The emphases in structure and content sketched out here form the axes of a system of co-ordinates with the help of which the labels often used for East European theology like 'traditionalism', 'antimodernism' and 'moralism' can be understood more appropriately.

1. Neoscholasticism

The ordained dissemination of neoscholasticism in the Catholic Church around the end of the nineteenth century was an intellectual attempt by the church to respond to the questions of modernity. As a system this theology was simplistic; it was not creative in content and was easy to learn and to teach. It was an *ancilla unitatis*, the handmaid of the unity of the church, which was defending itself against the world. Now when the church was visited with persecution in the region of East and Central Europe, to strengthen its oppressed unity it used the well-tried neoscholastic defensive theology. The beginning of another theology more disposed towards dialogue could develop at most in the prisons.

No critical assimilation of modernity in theology could take place in the time of the 'silent church'. It was isolated by the Iron Curtain from modern developments and also structurally incapable of such discussion.[12] Only after the political change was there a possibility for this. But the churches in this region in turn feel oppressed by liberalism, consumerism, freedom of opinion and a pluralism of values. They rarely find time and means for new theological reflection because it also touches on the level of the contents of revelation. Without a sure faith and a theology which is beyond discussion there are fears for the unity of the church and a new and assured position in society.

2. Traditionalism

Theologians and church people in Western countries can sometimes be heard to say that their colleagues in the East hold fundamentalist positions or at least cultivate relations with traditionalist trends. It is hard to judge

how far such assertions are correct. But it is certain that Western traditionalists show much understanding for those of like mind in the East because
they share the same attitude to the modern world and therefore are largely
agreed in their view of the status and mission of today's church. The difference between Western and Eastern traditionalists is above all a chronologi-
cal one. The former have remained traditionalists after centuries or at least
decades of modernization; the others have become traditionalists because
of the acute shock of modernization. The clear leaning of the East towards
tradition is moreover a healthy reaction to the forced separation of society
from its cultural roots and by no means represents merely a radical 'no' to
rising modernization. In grappling with the challenges which arise from
the restoration of society and the church, including theology, the living
memory of the traditions and a fearless grappling with the new time both
need to be cultivated at the same time. Here courage is required really to
pour new wine into new wineskins.

3. Underground theology

Just as the situation in society and the church differs widely in the region of
East (Central) Europe depending on the particular context, so too no clear
and simple answer can be given about the underground church or underground theology.[13] There are several reasons for this. One of the essential
characteristics of these non-public levels in the church is that they com-
municate only through channels of conspiracy. Even in one's own country
one only rarely knew the great variety of underground groups. The general
characteristics of the situation of an underground church include a politically enforced division into a part which is half-tolerated politically and a
part which is directly persecuted; the development of base structures and
strategies of communication in the underground; a great readiness to accept
the risks which the practice of faith brings with it; the revaluation of the role
of the laity and a proximity to areas of civil life. In this sense one can speak of
an underground church in the European part of the former Soviet Union, in
former Czechoslovakia and in Hungary, but not in Poland and former
Yugoslavia.

   If we want to have some idea of the theological praxis of this underground
organization, research depends on a few monographs by former members.
Here a romantic picture of the underground church as a place where most
Christians lived ready for martyrdom, disseminating a new church close to
the gospel and a new theology, is as much to be rejected as similar daydreams

about church and theology in the Third World. With due caution, however, it can be demonstrated from the sporadic sources that in these circles there was often more creativity and flexibility in theology, and that as a consequence more beginnings of a new theology can be found than at the 'official' level of the church, the level accepted by the state. Tomás Halik warns that three traditions of the underground church must not be lost: dialogue between faith and culture, the poverty of the church, and the link between the priestly ministry and a civil calling.[14] These three aspects point more or less in the direction of a well-considered contextuality of theology. These aspects need to be deepened further for an outline of a possible theology of the Second World.

IV. Theology of the Second World?

A theology of the Second World does not concentrate on the past, nor does it belong to it. Rather, it arises from theological reflection on the present-day culture of the region formerly dominated by Communism. One of its tasks is to expound again the basic themes of revelation and to find comprehensible language at this particular point. In my view its most important themes include: What do we understand by the power of God as we remember totalitarian power? What does freedom mean in connection with national self-determination and civil resistance? What kind of competence does the church have in the development of a post-Christian and a post-Communist culture? Finally, what language is fitting for the saints in a communication plagued with ideology? In addition, the theology of the most significant figures of the Communist-socialist past[15] must be worked out comparatively, including also the role of theological settings (e.g. the Berlin Conference) on which, in the countries concerned, for the most part a negative judgment is made.

The structures of theological work have altered since the change. Many priests' seminaries have been restructured as colleges of theology and have also opened their doors to lay people who want to study theology and/or religious education. Some theological places of education have investigated the possibilities of collaborating with state universities. Catholic universities with theological faculties have come into being. Freedom of expression has in principle made a theological dialogue possible. There is no longer any obstacle to taking part in international theological conferences and to international co-operation.

Nevertheless the new skins are often filled with old wine. The renewal of the theological disciplines along the lines of Vatican II and the Roman instructions to this effect is still in its infancy. Salvation-historical dogmatics, biblical hermeneutics, critical Christian social theory, practical theology and modern religious education are still looked upon fearfully. There is a desire and encouragement for theology to be a discipline with assured answers and not a discipline of open questions. The reports of many theologians from this region and also some statements by bishops give the impression that they look with some scepticism on the theological renewal. They see post-conciliar theology almost only as a plurality which is impossible to take in, and which weakens the unity of the church. The theological schemes from the times of the silent church, too, are very seldom integrated into the theological workshops and developed in them.

Hope for the theology of this region can be seen in the clearly intensified interest in religious questions which can be found among lay people and also in a wider public. But above all faith as lived out in the parishes and in renewal movements of various kinds is evoking a new kind of theology: a theology which can truly give an account of the hope of Christians in the new circumstances. Perhaps a theology of the Second World will develop. It seems indispensable for a repositioning of the Christian churches in the new situation.[16] It could also enrich the theological dialogue between the regions and cultures.

Translated by John Bowden

Notes

1. By Reform countries I understand the states of Eastern (Central) Europe which emerged after the political change of 1989/91 from satellite status to state autonomy.
2. Wilhelm Bernsdorf (ed.), *Wörterbuch der Soziologie*, Stuttgart 1969, 882–5; cf. 'Regionalism', in David L. Sills (ed.), *International Encyclopedia of the Social Sciences* 13, New York 1968, 377–82.
3. For a detailed account of this with precise sources see A.Máté-Tóth, *Theologie der Zweiten Welt*, Ostfildern 2000.
4. George Schöpflin, *Nations, Identity, Power*, London 2000; Endre Kiss, 'Ein Versuch, den post-sozialistischen Nationalismus zu interpretieren', in Robert Hettlage et al. (eds), *Kollektive Identität in Krisen. Ethnizität in Region, Nation, Europa*, Opladen 1997, 194–206. Further and more generally cf. Victor Conzeminus, 'Die Kirchen und der Nationalismus', in Peter Hünermann (ed.),

Das neue Europa. Herausforderungen für Kirche und Theologie, QD 144, Freiburg im Breisgau 1993.

5. Konrad Feiereis, 'Die Christen und die "Anderen". Das bleibende Problem des Atheismus und der missionarische Auftrag der Kirche', in C. März (ed.), *Die ganz alltagliche Freiheit*, 85–94; id., 'Geistige und religiöse Herausforderung in unserer Zeit', in W. Ernst (ed.), *Denkender Glaube im Geschichte und Gegenwart*, 170–6.

6. József Tischner, 'Glaube in düsteren Zeiten', in Hünermann (ed.), *Das neue Europa* (n.4), 211–27.

7. Elemér Hankiss, *East European Alternative*, Oxford 1990.

8. Cf. Hannes Gönner, *Die Stunde der Wahrheit*, Frankfurt am Main 1995.

9. 'Samisdat' (= self-publishing) was the name for writings which were not allowed by the state and therefore were publicized and disseminated underground.

10. Cf. A. Máté-Tóth, *Bulányi und die Bokor-Bewegung*, Vienna 1996; Tomás Halik, 'Verantwortung für die Untergrundkirche in der Tschechoslowakei', in id., *Du wirst das Angesicht der Erde erneuern. Kirche und Gesellschaft an der Schwelle zur Freiheit*, Leipzig 1993, 109–21; Oto Mádr, *Wie Kirche nich stirbt. Zeugnis aus bedrängten Zeiten der tchechicschen Kirche*, Leipzig 1993; id., 'Wahrheit als Waffe', *Diakonia* 24, 1993, 402–5.

11. Halik, 'Verantwortung für die Untergrundkirche' (n.10), and id., *Herder Korrespondenz* 5/1997.

12. Cf. Miklós Tomka, 'Strukturelle Konzilsresistenz', in Franz-Xaver Kaufmann and Arnold Zingerle (eds), *Vatikanum II. und Modernisierung*, Paderborn 1996, 291–313.

13. One speaks retrospectively about the underground church in Europe, as the totalitarian political structures which gave rise to it are already things of the past. Where these stuctures live on, there is also an underground church, e.g. in China or the house churches in Communist Vietnam.

14. Halik, 'Verantwortung für die Untergrundkirche' (n.10), 116–21.

15. Tamás Nyíri, Ferenc Gál (Hungary), Karol Wojtyla, Stefan Wyszynski (Poland), Tomislav Janko Sagi-Bunic (Croatia), Josef Zverina, Oto Mádr or Josef L. Hromadka (Czechia), to mention just some individual examples.

16. The framework and possibilities of this repositioning have been investigated since 1996 by the major research project Aufbruch (New Departures) under the direction of Professors Paul M. Zulehner, Vienna; Miklós Tomka, Budapest; and András Máté-Tóth, Zeged. See www.rel.u-szeged.hu/aufbruch. The results are being published in the series Gott nach dem Kommunismus, Schwabenverlag.

A Rise in Atheism?

ALBERT FRANZ

I. Consequences of the change

Has the fall of the Berlin Wall, which for decades divided Germany into two ideologically opposed worlds, and the dramatic end of the East-West conflict which came about as a result, boosted 'atheism' in Europe? Or has atheism, on the contrary, had a brake put on it by the 'new religion' which is evident everywhere?[1] However one may assess the revolutionary developments of the 1980s and 1990s, their significance for the wider development of society as a whole remains indisputable, in a way which extends far beyond the external drama. Here it is of central importance – even if this constantly risks being ignored in the 'Western' perspective – that the change brought about by the 1989/90 revolution did not just result in the fall of the world of Communism. Rather, the old division of the world into East and West and also 'the West' in the traditional sense have come to an end. The world, or at least Europe, has totally changed. What is new about the world after the change is not only that the society of the former West which has been exposed to a slow process of secularization can now also extend unhindered into the former East. Rather – and this is something which goes far deeper – the new element consists in the fact that with the collapse of the external frontiers, East and West are mixing in many ways, even if from an external perspective the image of society in the former East is being visibly Westernized. What new significant spiritual and religious constellations this will produce will become evident only gradually, but its scope can hardly be overestimated.

Thus the development of religion and belief in God in twenty-first century Europe has not just been preceded by the gradually developing and complex process of secularization in the former West;[2] rather, this horizon and content also included ideological atheism and the religionless and anti-religious ideology of the Communist ideology which has collapsed politically. It would be naïve to think that with the end of the East-West conflict all this is really finished and completely done away with. Whatever the processes of the reorientation of Europe which began with the change in 1989 and is still far from completion may bring, at any rate they pose new challenges for theology and church, previously undreamed of and thought to be hardly possible. These include, first of all, recognition and acceptance of this new context which is being formed and (self-)critical reflection on it. Only in this way will it be possible to discover the place of God in the Europe of the twenty-first century and thus also to answer the question where we must indeed speak of a 'rise in atheism' and what this could mean for Christian belief in God and thus for the task of the church today and tomorrow.[3]

I cannot give any comprehensive analyses here, let alone suggest answers. I shall merely discuss in a very concrete way, from the perspective of a systematic theologian in the philosophical faculty of a 'Technical University', with a specific reference to concrete experiences in the Eastern part of now united Germany, the question how far in this scientific context, in this specific world, it is possible to speak of a rise in atheism after the change.[4] I leave it to the critical reader to reflect how far this is to be seen as a paradigm for other contexts.

II. 'Scientific atheism' and the atheism of science

Surveys and statistics confirm what can continually be experienced in everyday life. Among the population of the former DDR, people have got used to atheism; the reason for this is that they have essentially (though not exclusively) been influenced by the elites trained in this kind of thinking during the period of socialism.[5] There is a kind of widespread godlessness which almost as a matter of course determines the mentality of people and institutions. This would hardly have arisen without the ideological model of 'scientific atheism': attempts have been made, using considerable pressure, to implant this model at all levels of education and through the communication of knowledge in the thought and sensibilities of several generations. However, relative success was achieved here only because the ground had been prepared by a process of alienation from the church and Christianity (going back to the Enlightenment) and the 'atheizing' of large areas of the population in former Central Germany. That seems to explain talk of the 'phenomenon of mass acceptance of atheism' in the society of the former DDR.[6]

The downfall of the political and ideological system of socialism in the DDR in no way shook this fundamental accord with atheism. Far less can it be said that – with few exceptions – the revival of any form of belief in God is recognizable, even if church circles have occasionally longed for this – having seen the churches filled by demonstrators in the days and weeks of the change in 1989. Manifestly many people feel that at least the atheistic components of the Marxist-Leninist ideology have remained (though this ideology has failed both in practice and theoretically), as still valuable insights which can be justified by critical thought. This atheism is then accepted all the more gratefully as one of the few elements which could be salvaged in the new social and scientific context. Thus the conviction of atheism, which under the new conditions is in this way legitimated as scientific, is regarded by many people as virtually a bridge between the present reality and the old system which has collapsed. Indeed it is an important link in a person's own biography, which is often felt to be broken, and thus serves as a proof that not all one's former convictions were wrong.

However, this presupposes that reality after the change offers points of contact for this atheistic understanding of self and world which is in no way identical with the 'scientific atheism' of the Communist ideology, though it emerged from this context and penetrated deep into the consciousness. Now that the East-West conflict has been overcome, atheism of an 'Eastern' stamp in fact meets up with a 'Western' understanding of self and the world which, while being incomparably more differentiated and varied, indeed contradictory and quite lacking in homogeneity, in this specific form contains not only marginal atheistic components. These components now appear as important interfaces between the Eastern and the Western consciousness and in this specific context take on increased significance; in turn they are considerably reinforced from their side. At all events this is true of the academic world, and especially of the humane and cultural sciences, which during and after the reconstruction of universities could in practice flow into the East without hindrance, when a vacuum formed in the course of the development away from the old Marxist/Leninist ideology and its institutions. Now if this is the case, such a rise of atheism cannot be regarded as the legacy of the former East – at least, not in a one-sided way. Rather, as a result of this process it becomes clearer than anywhere else how decisively and fundamentally a completely atheistic understanding of self and world could become the presupposition and the almost universally accepted horizon of science and other academic study outside the context of Marxist-Leninist ideology, i.e. in the former West. So much is that the case that today there is hardly any reflection that goes beyond it.

Theology should not be afraid of noting this; it should not be misled into over-hasty defensive reactions but react soberly. Such an attitude could sharpen focus more clearly on essentials, not least in the present discussions about the status of theology as a university discipline.[7]

In this way, first of all we see that 'East' and 'West' are not two completely alien worlds. To begin with, there are as it were figures and elements of a common history of thought and mentality which are also characterized by atheistic currents (though with very different emphases).[8] Thus because of its origin in the 'scientific' ideology of Marxism and Leninism, atheism of the 'Eastern' kind is and was a system of convictions which primarily refers back to an alleged basis in reason; from this perspective religion is primarily regarded as superseded because it has been shown up to be the product of human beings and their (alienated) needs. Here Christianity in particular is to be regarded as refuted because its premises are not scientifically tenable (e.g. the world as creation and not as a process of evolution). Over against this stood and stands atheism of the 'Western' kind, for which God seems initially to have disappeared less from reason than from memory.[9] This certainly means that in 'scientific atheism' God is explicitly and pro-grammatically denied and the non–existence of God is claimed to have been proved in principle; on the other hand, in the thought of the individual sciences and philosophy the forgotten God no longer appears, simply for methodological reasons. In this context obviously the question of God as a whole is increasingly thought and felt to be obsolete, albeit in a more diffuse way. This provides the conditions for both genres of atheism finally to meet at the decisive point: a final farewell must be said to God; in the end there-fore God is not so much unnecessary as incompatible with critical thought.

Niklas Luhmann, who is often seen as a magisterial authority in circles and contexts of research where this notion is dominant, sums up such think-ing in a succinct and programmatic way; he thus becomes the normative paradigm when, for example, he thinks that the history of the question of God is wholly a matter for sociology (at the same time, however, claiming a comprehensive competence at interpretation). 'Tradition had externalized interest in an infallible description and called the corresponding position God.'[10] Accordingly the talk of 'autopoiesis' as a 'production of the system by itself',[11] which is central to Luhmann's thought, is more than a merely methodological approach. It stands for no less than a kind of world system, indeed for an almost stubborn immanentist metaphysic.

Within such a horizon there is in fact no longer talk of an absolute which goes beyond this and is independent of it (thus of the real God), because there is either no longer any interest in it or it has disappeared from memory. That is the case where Luhmann is simply accepted in an external way and applied more or less uncritically to individual pieces of research. Furthermore, in principle it is no longer even possible here to talk of God as a real problem. Here God can only be misunderstood in the sense of a mere moment, an extrapolation of the ultimately groundless, because autopoietic, events of reality should God return in the memory, though hardly by chance. Necessarily the word 'God' here is only a metaphor. However, this God-metaphor is no longer open to the possibility that God is spoken of metaphorically only because God cannot really be grasped in human language. Rather, here the metaphor stands for the fact that with 'God' a merely human reality is transferred into a language-game which is created by human beings and then called 'theology' or 'religion'.

Such findings will provoke a theology which allows itself to be impressed and satisfied by the mere use of the word 'God' in an academic and scientific context, and contentedly suggests that 'religion' is growing. Such a theology is less interested in what all this may stand for if it recognizes in it only a certain potential for theology to legitimate itself as a discipline.[12] However, academic theology should resolutely and critically note the atheism which is woven into such thinking and feeling. It should face the new challenges bound up with this and not content itself with daydreams, as if such an atheism in academic and scientific disciplines – because of the alleged differentiations in it – should be taken less seriously than the ideological atheism which has collapsed, or as if it were compensated for by an increase in the mentality impregnated with religion in contexts outside the academic and scientific world.

III. Theo-logy: the science of God in the face of the challenge from atheism

The development described here can show clearly enough the danger to which a way of thinking which is immanentist in approach is particularly exposed. In the end, after all, contrary to its own perception of itself, it will divert into being an apparently academic, but in truth crypto-ideological, atheism with a pseudo-religious claim. For example, the uncritical claim to totality which is almost a necessary element in Luhmann's concept of autopoiesis is not even watered down by the formula which runs: God has nothing to do with thinking but with a 'faith' which is alleged to be abso- lutely different, and this God (then to sum up the whole thing 'rationally') is to be understood merely as an aesthetic phenomenon. God is really done away with.[13] In terms of cultural theory or the hermeneutics of history, legitimate interest can certainly be shown in the notion of 'God'; however, in the end God is no longer a substantive problem which could specifically challenge scientific reality. But if God is marginalized in this way, the result, whether intended or unintended, is a metaphysical judgment not only on God but as it were on the autopoietic character of the reality of the world and human beings, behind which it is impossible to go. But here theology has, for example, to ask critically whether such a tendency towards pseudo-theologizing can be avoided at all unless the human desire to know is firmly focussed on truth, unity and the totality of what is. Can an apparently critical scientific contemporary consciousness which corresponds to the general standard still be concerned with this and in a stubbornly immanentist way insist that it cannot make enquiries beyond this point because our capacity for knowledge is indisputably finite, conditioned in many ways, and indeed broken? On the other hand, does not the phenomenon of the 'new religion' that goes along with this immanentizing and atheizing of the scientific consciousness and the public consciousness which is essentially shaped by it show that the human openness which is forced out of such a rationality gives a living response: for truth, unity and totality, and thus for transcendence, for God?[14]

These questions cannot be discussed here, far less can answers be suggested. However, they should all make it clear that the constellations of problems indicated with the word 'atheism' are less resolved than ever today, after the change. Nor is it sufficient to counter these problems with more emotional, purely 'religious' or pastoral and practical strategies, whether these are fundamentalist and aggressive or stamped more by indifference or even resignation. Certainly the external power of ideological atheism has been broken. But atheistic thought is in fact far from really being at an end, at any rate in practical scientific work. It still implies an ideological tendency to claim comprehensive truth, however much this may lie under the surface. After the change it seems to be asserting itself all the more strongly in a new garb and a new quality, at least in the scientific consciousness. But that means that academic theology, and also a pastoral work which is conscious of the context, faces a challenge from atheism which is all the stronger.

Be this as it may, the question of God in former East Germany, and not only here, is again being felt as an intellectual challenge. But the theological reaction to this challenge cannot and must not be to set pseudo-theological pseudo-solutions to the problem of God from the side of scholarly theology against others which similarly claim final validity. Everything will depend on our really keeping open the question of God, both theoretically and practically, and thus taking seriously the person who is deeply stamped by present-day rationality and therefore seeks comprehensive truth. Here we must use all our rationality to see that God is allowed and not ruled out from the start or trivialized in a pseudo-critical way. However, we shall not succeed here if theology assimilates itself as closely as possible to a scientific consciousness which then gives it all the more of a right to scientific existence provided that it does not raise the specific problem of God as a substantive problem which deeply challenges reason and intellect, but allows itself to be assigned as its specific subject for example the culture and history of Christian faith or the phenomenon of religious consciousness. Nor, however, will it succeed if, in order to escape such levelling down, church praxis and theology retreat into the ghetto of a world of faith which is apparently unassailable because it has become fundamentalistic.[15]

The theological, or more specifically the Catholic theological, tradition faces this challenge when it speaks of *fides quaerens intellectum*, of a faith which seeks unity, and finds this search a distinctive feature of theology. Only if present-day theology does not fall short of this, but with the inexorability of e.g. Anselm of Canterbury faces the problem of atheism, which deeply disturbs faith and thought but drives both forward – only if here it sees its most authentic cause, which is not forced on it from outside, will it be able to claim to be a distinctive discipline which can be differentiated from other disciplines and at the same time is indispensable. Only in this way will theology be able to introduce 'faith' as a relevant factor, along with its specific concept of 'thinking', as an indispensable perspective on the theoretical discourse of the present.[16] Should theology today fail here in undercutting its own claim, then it puts the existence of theology and the future of the Christian church at risk. And if it does that, it contributes to the fact that even after the change, however one may assess the rise of atheism since then, the age of dangerous ideological thinking is not yet at an end.

Translated by John Bowden

Notes

1. Klaus-Peter Jörns, *Die neuen Gesichter Gottes. Was die Menschen heute wirklich glauben*, Munich 1997, is informative here and gives statistical material.
2. Cf. Karl Gabriel, *Christentum zwischen Tradition und Postmoderne*, Freiburg im Breisgau, Basel and Vienna ⁶1998.

3. For the themes of 'Theology in Europe' or 'Belief in God between Tradition and Modernity', see the bulletin *ET. Zeitschrift für Theologie in Europa* 1998/1 and 2.

4. Since 1993 I have been Professor of Systematic Theology (Catholic) at the Technical University of Dresden. As well as training teachers of religion, my main task has been to give theology a presence in this university context. The term atheism is used here in the general definition proposed by Walter Kasper: 'Atheism has to be regarded as the view which denies any form of the divine or absolute which is not simply identical with human beings and with the world of our empirical experience and its immanent principles', *The God of Jesus Christ*, New York and London 1984, 19.

5. Thus Wolf Krötke, *Die christliche Kirche und der Atheismus. Überlegungen zur Konfrontation der Kirchen in den neuen Bundesländern mit einer Masserscheinung: Wege zum Einverständnis. Festschrift für Christoph Demke*, ed. Michael Beintker, Eberhard Jüngel und Wolf Krötke, Leipzig 1997, 159–71: 160.

6. Ibid., 159.

7. Cf. here Albert Franz (ed.), *Bindung an die Kirche oder Autonomie? Theologie im gesellschaftlichen Diskurs*, Freiburg im Breisgau 1999.

8. Cf. Winfried Schröder, *Ursprünge des Atheismus. Untersuchungen zur Metaphysik- und Religionskritik des 17. und 18. Jahrhunderts*, Stuttgart-Bad Cannstatt 1998.

9. Cf. Anton W. J. Houtepen, *God – An Open Question. Thinking of God in a Godless Time*, London 2000.

10. In *Die Gesellschaft der Gesellschaft. Erster Teilband*, Frankfurt am Main 1997, 89.

11. Ibid., 97.

12. Cf. Klaus Hofmeister and Lothar Bauerochse (eds.), *Die Zukunft der Religion. Spurensicherung an der Schwelle zum 21. Jahrhunderts*, Würzburg 1999.

13. For Luhmann cf. Heinz-Theo Homann, *Das funktionale Argument. Konzepte und Kritik funktionlogischer Religionsbegründung*, Paderborn, etc. 1997, and Matthias Woiwode, *Heillose Religion? Eie fundamentaltheologische Untersuchung zur funktionalen Religionstheorie Niklas Luhmanns*, Münster 1997.

14. Cf. Hans-Joachim Höhn (ed.), *Krise der Immanenz, Religion an der Grenze der Moderne*, Frankfurt am Main 1996.

15. So the classic *demonstratio religiosa* as a rational engagement with the question of God in so far as it is raised in the context of the contemporary critique for religion deserves renewed and deeper attention.

16. Cf. Albert Franz, 'Der Wahrheitsanspruch der Theologie', in Karl Homann and Ilona Riedel-Spangenberger (ed.), *Welt-Heuristik des Glaubens*, Gütersloh 1997, 26–46, and Klaus Müller, *Fundamentaltheologie. Fluchtlinien und gegenwärtige Herausforderungen*, Regensburg 1998, especially the contributions by Edmund Arens, 59–76, and, by contrast, Klaus Müller, 77–100.

Social Upheaval and the Phenomenon of Atheism: Two Challenges

MILOSLAV CARDINAL VLK

It is more than a decade since Communism collapsed as a result of the 'velvet revolution'.[1] At that time the complete freedom which the whole of society had long awaited and fought for opened up. In their euphoria many people thought that the new freedom would renew everything and everyone. Many people hoped that Communism was finished and that now all the forces that had fought against it would collaborate. For the most part we overlooked the fact that Communism was somehow preserved in the heads and hearts of everyone, even the anti-Communists. We did not want to note that the negative legacy of Communist indoctrination has serious consequences lasting for generations, and that the transformation, the change of heart, will take a long time. That is true for both political society and for the church.

In modern Czech history perhaps the church never enjoyed such great sympathy as it did in the time of the velvet revolution. At that time, at the moment of the collapse of atheistic Communism, people sensed the true, spiritual face of the church. Everyone saw the church as the powerful bearer of the truth and of love; these were the very values which were to prevail over the lie and hatred, as the chief motto of this revolution ran. The collapse of Communism was understood at that time above all as the victory of good over evil.

But most leading political personalities had unrealistic, 'ideal' notions of society, of human beings, of faith and also of the church. The people of that period – one should really say 'we' – had the false and naïve notion that now it was finally time to change everything for the better and that the new order could be established with the wave of a magic wand. Such a splendid and unrealistic naivety was applied to many spheres of life: to the church and its capabilities, and to society, which at that time – as some people thought – could quite suddenly open up to faith.

Here people noticed that the church is not just a political organism and that spiritual values cannot simply be conveyed with preaching; they have to be 'inculcated'. And it is impossible to 'inculcate' values without personally being deeply rooted in Christ. It is possible only on the basis of a living testimony and in a long laborious process, for which the majority of the church, as a whole, was not at all prepared after forty years of Communism. It was also forgotten that the little scattered elite groups which had the necessary experiences and knew the issues could not manage to carry through this spiritual revolution as 'gently' as the political revolution.

The churches found it far more difficult than they expected to define their standpoint in this process of transformation. The forty years of their enforced ghetto situation and their almost total exclusion from public, social and political life weakened them considerably, so that they could not live up to their calling of being communion. At the same time they are also burdened with all the negative phenomena of civil society.

The Second Vatican Council went largely unrealized in the post-Communist countries. To put this quite critically: people did not renew the spirit but merely changed the forms. Certainly the Catholic Church must not transform the gospel or the liturgy or the sacrament or the texts. The cross of Christ remains its centre – after the change as before it. But together with the other churches it must find a new standpoint in the democratic constitutional state and in pluralistic society and a new inner structure as well as new methods for its work. It must develop from a church of the clergy into a church of the people of God, with active laity who engage in associations and church movements. The *aggiornamento* called for by Pope John XXIII, i.e. an appropriate change, is one of the demands of the hour. This change must take place in the presence of the church in society, in its catechesis and its religious instruction in schools, its pastoral work in state institutions, its contributions in the spheres of education and social work, its charitable activities, its presence in public institutions and not least in its organizations for study and training. That calls not only for great material means but also for wisdom, imagination, sensitivity and obviously for more time than was first assumed.

In this situation there are now disappointments on many sides which again are being formulated in terms of a false, one-sided and sweeping assessment: the church has failed and forfeited its one chance. Psychologically that is quite understandable: people look for a scapegoat and an excuse for their own failure in the economic and political disappointments. They look for it in others.

The present tension in society and the political instability of recent years are the consequences above all of that condition in which the spiritual dimension dominates the economy. The twofold danger of this situation consists in the combination of the strength of the old mentality in us and the weakness of the mechanisms which are to protect the new freedom. The 'old' evil still remains in us and very often prevents us from dealing rightly with the new freedom. The inner poisoning remains as the result of systematic brainwashing. How else can we explain why such a high proportion of the population (empirical research speaks of a third or even more of the population of Eastern Central Europe) prefers the former system to the present?

The mendacious separation of words from reality, so typical of the Communist ideology, can only be healed by a patient search for the truth about men and women which really makes us free (cf. John 8.32), and accordingly we must learn to act as free men and women. First we must liberate ourselves from the collectivism and passivity in thought which prevent us from giving ourselves unaccustomed challenges. We are still to used to 'someone from above' thinking for us, and are often afraid of making independent decisions. It is necessary to recognize that in public affairs there is no longer 'us' and 'them', the way in which the 'people' and the ruling party used to be divided. On the contrary, today everyone has to bear responsibility. It is time to put an end to 'inward emigration' into the narrow circle of family or acquaintances. The passive attitude is convenient, but it deprives us of a good deal of freedom.

Nor is the theory of class struggle and class hatred dead in our everyday practice. The hatred is now directed against those who in some way are different from us, and often it takes the guise of racial hatred and xenophobia. There is a perceptible concern for selfish or group interests in ethnic and national intolerance. Intolerance of the 'religious minority' – of the church – also belongs in this area. This intolerance was developed by the Communists and has reappeared in recent years. The church has been described as an institution which is 'against the nation', and this attitude has also in part been passed down to the youth.

Immediately after 1989 there was a structural reform within the Catholic Church. At the same time new bishops were nominated to sees which had often been vacant for decades. The Conference of Bishops was established in Czechoslovakia. The religious orders and also various activities – previously designated 'illegal' or 'semi-legal' – appeared in public again. With surprising vigour the religious press began to satisfy the hunger for spiritual literature. Caritas was able to become a living church structure. Soon the first church schools came into being. Many good things were done and the church gained more freedom than ever before. Nevertheless, particularly to the eyes of observers standing outside it, it largely remains on the periphery of society. The way of Christians out of the ghetto is full of difficulties and seems to be longer and more laborious than was hoped for immediately after November 1989.

In fact the church in all post-Communist countries (with the exception of Poland) not only decreased numerically but also lost political influence and economic power. All that inevitably governed the change in mentality. In the Czech Republic, in my opinion we still have not sufficiently taken account of the fact that we have become a minority of less than 30%. Not only the laity – particularly the older ones – but also some priests and especially we bishops must take account of this. After the collapse of Communism it was hoped that in the new freedom people would fill the churches again. That was a great disappointment, because the new freedom has fostered old material hopes, or better the temptation to achieve by one's own efforts the paradise that was not attained earlier. Neither the political pressure under Communism nor freedom bring forth the fruit of new Christians. Only the testimony of renewed Christians produces this.

To the realization that we are a small flock must be added the insight that in ourselves we are no better than the others. Perhaps one learned in Communism, but also even before that, to despise the others, especially the atheists. The change in awareness called for can help towards a new identity: that we are no longer a ruling church but a serving church, which will change the world by the testimony of its life.

There are some time-lags on this way of repentance. As under Communism, so too today – under other conditions – there are groups with different views. They cause the polarization of our church scene and put a brake on the real renewal of life. The first group thinks it necessary to remain in the past, to change as little as possible, because at that time there were no problems, nor was there decay in the church. Sometimes they also blame the Council, especially liturgical reform. They seek confirmation, refuge and protection in various appearances of Mary. They are characterized by anxiety, especially anxiety about the spirit and the influence of the West, where in fact one can also note deep shadows in the church sphere. In addition there is anxiety about 'freemasons' or other spectres in the church. As to their 'method', there is a concern to rescue the church 'for the Lord' on their own initiative and in their own strength, their own 'power'. That is how people work, especially in traditionalist areas: an authentic renewal is hindered. There are many shades in this group, from the admirers of the old theology to the supporters of Lefèbvre.

The other pole is composed of those who want to open up the church more to the influence of Western currents. Some of them want to save the church above all through the spirit of freedom and through democracy, as they also see the great good that exists in the church in the West. Their activity sometimes reinforces the anxiety of the first group. Each group influences the other.

With the polarization, however, it has not proved possible to carry on a lively dialogue and to discuss beyond the two standpoints. There have been quite a few successful efforts to bring both sides to the same table, but often the different poles merely skulk in their own spheres. Attempts are made to widen this sphere and to reinforce one's own position. And that brings us back to the beginning: the exercise of power from the position of one's own truth, the 'power of truth', not the service of truth.

We do not manage to engage with and have a dialogue with those of other opinions. Personal opinions are often turned into ideologies and the art of mutually respectful dialogue is very rare. We have no practice in dialogue, because this is also completely lacking in Communism – in both society and the church. This mentality is even stronger among the bishops, who for forty years were compelled to rely on themselves, always to make their own decisions and as it were be their own 'bishop'. They lived by the customary theological attitude of the priest as it developed in the course of the Middle Ages: the priest has in the church the spiritual power that comes from Christ. This attitude was reinforced under the influence of the Communist policy: this wanted a priest remote from the people. The perspective of the last supper, the footwashing, still remains in the far distance – also because of the age of the priests. Here the legacy of the first group mentioned above lives on. But there is also the lack of a systematic programme which trains people in the new mentality.

The heaviest burden that we bear with us from the past, however, is the absence of true transcendent values and immanentism in life. I see here a warning sign that the harsh lesson of Communism was not perhaps enough for us. Earlier there was the institutionalized truth of Marxist materialism, which had removed any transcendence. But what happened after the political change? Theoretical materialism was given up; its place was taken by consumer thinking and the effort to consume in an ever 'better' way. In this way the 'vertical' dimension of transcendence was removed by a 'horizontal' one. As a result the void remained; indeed it even grew into a vicious circle: one needs more and more yet is ever more unsatisfied.

In Czechoslovakia after 1948 the ground was 'ideologically' well prepared for the rise of Communistic atheism. Particularly among a large part of the intellectuals one encountered a widely secularized way of thinking. The materialist ideology was not totally uncongenial to people who thought in this way; the official state atheism was none other than the climax of the 'liberation' from God which had already begun with the Enlightenment and went further in the following period.

But at the same time it was also the 'liberation' from principles of ethics and morality which are anchored not only in the Bible but also in the human heart and in human nature. All human beings have within them the principle of love, to love and to be loved. The starting point of atheism was precisely the opposite, i.e. the doctrine of class hatred which steadily also penetrated the hearts and the lives of individuals and even families. Children were brought up in this hatred from their schooldays on. Among the great variety of 'class enemies', believers were a very popular target in this education in hatred. On the basis of these principles of education it could come about that a teacher asked the children in a class which of them still believed in God. Some said that they did, and the teacher told the other children to mock them because they were 'backward obscurantists'. But such a way of behaving was also a way of covering one's own mistakes and soothing one's own conscience. Could such a form of behaviour, practised for decades, fail to have consequences for people's souls? Can one simply eradicate it in a few years? In a recent programme on Czech public television the member of a youth group openly called the church a 'criminal organization' . . .

Atheism has utterly denied God the Father, the Creator, as a ground of human dignity, but in this way the brotherhood proclaimed by the French Revolution, which later became a 'socialist brotherhood' among individuals and peoples, has lost its foundation. Without a common father people cannot feel themselves brothers! One can presuppose with an almost mathematical logic that any 'brotherhood' without God falls victim to totalitarianism. Wasn't the proof that Communism gave us sufficient? We should not forget that not to understand one's own history means to be condemned to repeat it.

There is certainly no quick and simple therapy for the sickness of atheism. But the development of secularization here is on our side. Some decades ago a well-known sociologist of religion 'forged' a dogma about the irreversibility of the process of secularization. Under the pressure of developments he had to revoke this dogma when he saw that the religious people which secularism leaves behind are again calling on God. Today's secularized men and women are seeking, seeking God, seeking answers for their questions about the true meaning of life. But the therapy from our side must be unconditionally radical and begin precisely where atheism has done the greatest damage. There are two spheres in particular here. Atheism has destroyed not only the image of God but also the sense of community and brotherhood in the human heart. So there is a restoration of God from the periphery to the centre of human life, a restoration of the true image of God (not a caricature which is often confused with this image), and a renewal of the *communio* of the church. The church must become a sign of God's presence, a place where God is present despite all human weakness, as a promised gift – for humankind.

Here we must make a true conversion so that all talk about God grows from our relationship with God. We must strive for personal holiness, because 'the church can survive only where there are saints'. Only living saints are the true and convincing martyrs – witnesses. In *Evangelii Nuntiandi* 41, Paul VI says of them: 'Modern man listens more willingly to witnesses than to teachers . . . and if he does listen to teachers it is because they are witnesses.'

There can be no doubt that the traditional Christians in our churches and those who live for themselves are no exceptions. The truth that Christ did not come for the healthy but for the sick is not being taken seriously! God came for the unbelievers. He is their God! We must still grow up a lot to become witnesses in this sense. That is the first presupposition for tearing down the many prejudices against the church which still exist. We can hasten this process only by acknowledging our own mistakes, by asking for forgiveness for our failures and by patient dialogue with the whole of society.

The true image of God and the true church communion constructed in accordance with this image belong very closely together. The Constitution on the Sacred Liturgy *Sacrosanctum Concilium* 7 mentions, alongside the eucharistic presence of Christ, also his presence in the word of Holy Scripture and the midst of those who are assembled in his name (Matt. 18.20). Those are two important traces to follow, because they make Jesus 'visible'. They are at the same time also two undisputed points at which we can meet Christians of all confessions and together bear witness to the world. The living and risen Christ among us is the only way in which atheists can 'experience' in a 'secularized' way, that is in a visible and 'tangible' way.

From my personal experience I can demonstrate the power of Jesus to 'raise up churches' in small communities. When in the times of unfreedom every activity and structure of the church was paralysed, the presence of Jesus in these small groups of young people, families, priests, spread everywhere, and gave them all the courage to persist and continue in their life by faith. Even now, perhaps more than before, we meet the 'Emmanuel', the 'near God', the 'God with us', the Holy One *par excellence*, who can give life to the structures of the church as they renew themselves and make the church an authentic *koinonia*; who can stimulate Christians to effective service of others, to *diakonia*; and raise them up to shared praise of the father in true *leiturgia*.

And finally, if one imagines the image of God in the face of present-day atheism, one must not forget the figure of the one who 'was like God . . . and who became a slave and in the likeness of human beings' (Phil. 2.6–7), Jesus the crucified and forsaken one. In his kenosis on the cross he even identified himself with theism. In him at the same time we encounter the deepest abyss of that human pain and the supreme image of the divine: in the moment where he is most human he is also most the love of God. Non-believers, often unconsciously, seek such a God – not the just God who judges. The church which wants to carry on an effective dialogue with atheism must follow this 'forsaken' God and fill up in its body 'what is still lacking in the suffering of Christ' (Col. 1.24). Only in this way can it give a more authentic testimony.

The cross is the point where all challenges to the renewal and the mission of the church come together. The only challenge is loyalty to the cross: to discover, accept and love the cross. In the time of the dictatorship this way was perhaps more visible and easier to find. The cross of freedom comes in varied, hidden and deceptive forms, but it always remains the only way for the church in this world, among all the political and economic regulations. In the cross too we have the eternal ground for our true optimism, because it is the certain way of the resurrection. It is also a way of testing whether we rely on ourselves, our own strength and achievements, or whether we have chosen the way of weakness which relies on God.

Translated by John Bowden

Note

1. The revised text of a lecture given at the symposium 'Religion in the Reform Countries of Eastern (Central) Europe' in Vienna on 24 January 1999 under the auspices of the international research project 'New Departures'. For the first results of this movement cf. Miklós Tomka and Paul M.Zulehner, *Religion in den Reformländern Ost(Mitte) Europas*, Ostfildern 1999.

Pastoral Work and the Shock of
Modernization

JANUSZ MARIANSKI

I shall examine the problem of religion and the church in the Polish society and church of the 1990s from a particular socio-political and socio-cultural context. The keywords are: a changed socio-economic situation with the collapse of so-called real socialism; an end of the monopoly of power of the Communist Party, which could not meet the demands of the time for civilization and culture; and the removal of Marxist totalitarianism.

In the theoretical conception of the Communist state there was no place for the church as an independent institution with an influence on public life. However, it emerged strengthened and independent from its confrontation with the totalitarian system – as a 'sign which is spoken against'; it could reinforce its influence on the nation and the values which determined its spiritual face. Religious faith played an important role not only in the preservation and even strengthening of the identity of the Polish nation, but also in the struggle for freedom and its attainment.

In the socio-political realm we are in the transition from a central command economy to the market economy; from a bureaucratic-totalitarian system to a democratic system; from a monocentric social order (which controls almost all spheres of life through the central authorities) to a poly-centric social order (with many centres of power and responsibility); from an unfree society (which has been robbed of its subjectivity) to a civil society (which possesses its subjectivity); from a state-controlled society to a self-chosen society; from a community of fate to a community of choice. The outlines of a pluralistic society are arising in all spheres of social life. We are overcoming visible 'structures of sin' in the old system; here there are inevitable tensions between the desire to erect a new social order and all the negative attitudes which form an unavoidable legacy from the past. These manifold changes, which are accompanied by numerous tensions, indeed moral conflicts, are further overlaid with the cultural changes in connection with the development of science and culture, with technological progress and the development of the media. Church and society are experiencing a shock of modernization.

I. Hypotheses about religion and the church in a modernizing society

In the context of the socio-cultural changes of the pluralistic society which is coming into being and in the light of the prognoses and prophecies of a total crisis for religion (the so-called wave of secularization) which is allegedly coming to us, the question arises of the opportunities for the sense of religion which revived in the 1980s. In the twenty-first century, are we threatened by a galloping de-Christianization or at least a creeping secularization, or must we reckon with a change in the model of religion and the quest for new patterns of religious life? Has the overcoming of real socialism in Poland resulted in a diminution of the significance and role of the church in society? How will it function under the conditions of pluralism and a pragmatic democracy? Is the Christian colouring of our culture being maintained? Or in the foreseeable future will Poland perhaps become a mission country, with a vanishing Christian tradition, as is the case in many countries of Western Europe? Do religion and the church remain an integral element in this modernizing society? Will not the selectivity which is characteristic of Polish religion – in accordance with a tendency to be observed in Western countries – lead to the privatization and subjectivization of faith?

There are many detailed diagnoses and prognoses of Polish Catholicism at the beginning of the 1990s in scholarly and more popular works. Many authors think that in connection with the introduction of democratic procedures in the political sphere, the market mechanisms in the economy and the extension of freedom in all spheres of life, Poland is taking on the fundamental characteristics of the Western European social order, and that there is thus a wide-ranging secularization of individual and social life (the hypothesis of the imitative transformation of religious life). Here Western secularization would be the desired goal of the evolution in religion which is taking place. According to this hypothesis the pattern of Western de-Christianization will be repeated in Poland, to the degree that our country becomes a modern, highly-developed, advanced and prosperous society – in other words when Poland 'joins' Europe.

A future weakening or even collapse of Catholicism is also prophesied by those who see the strength of religion and the church in Poland almost exclusively as a commitment to tradition and nationalism. When the role of traditional, socio-cultural and especially political motivations diminishes, the religion based on such motivations (and thus the whole of national religion) must become weaker. According to these views, the increasing religious feeling in Polish society in the 1980s had above all a socio-political character and served to demonstrate non-religious (e.g. national) values. The church could strengthen its social and moral authority only because it collaborated with the political opposition movements (by way of political religion).

Many sociologists emphasize that Polish religion is conventional, a matter of habit, traditional and not wholly authentic, without a deeper religious knowledge and deeper motivations, but instead with a strong emphasis on ritual and the religious practices enjoined by the church (an ostentatious participation in religious actions). According to these judgments, religion is understood to be important in categories relating to festivals and the cult: it has no respect for moral challenges, but by contrast it is alive in its popular, ritual and patriotic features. According to some sociologists, alongside small enclaves of so-called enlightened Catholics the elements of a popular belief are dominant: people take part predominantly in particular mass occasions, without the elements of deeper ethical reflection and 'metaphysical' sensibilities. The national church, which did great service as an advocate of the inalienable rights of human beings and their dignity in the battle against Communism, was certainly one of the most effective factors in liberating people from the system of totalitarian dependence, but its opportunities in a pluralistic society are not very high. A far-reaching secularization is unavoidable (the hypothesis of the collapse of popular religion and the national church).

According to a third standpoint the church and religion are in transition from a totalitarian society to a democratic society. These changes, too, will take place in a differentiated way and in different directions; particular functions of religion and the church will be deepened and at the same time diminished (the hypothesis of the multi-dimensionality of the changes in religion and the church).

We must take account of a differentiation of the genres and variants of religious life, in different dimensions. The more new interests and needs of a pluralistic nature develop which were previously suppressed, the stronger will be the effect of the 'ideological market' in which the religious offer is only one of many. The various group interests will articulate themselves increasingly clearly. Perhaps the highest religious values will appear less in public life. But that does not mean that they no longer have any influence on social life or that religion no longer has any connection with the culture of the nation.

II. The Catholic Church in a changing society

A decisive feature of the character of Polish religion is the tendency for Poles to manifest their religious self-understanding and to take part in worship *en masse*. Even in those strata of society which traditionally distance themselves from the church, atheism is no longer in fashion. By contrast, people in particular circles have become accustomed to expressing their distance from the institutional church in various ways.

Sociological investigations indicate that the vast majority of Polish society (at least formally) identifies with the Catholic Church. Around 90% of all Poles declare their belief in God or at least in a higher power. The vast majority take part more or less regularly in religious practices. Almost all children are baptized and go to First Communion (the percentage of un-baptized children is under 2%).

As to the quality of the religion of Poles, we can establish above all that here to a large degree religion is very much an eclectic matter, which to some extent is inconsistent and 'incomplete'; in the moral sphere it also has marked individualistic tendencies. Religion coexists with moral permissive-ness. The ongoing socio-economic and political crisis could lead to a further collapse of ethics in Polish society and produce pathological features in many spheres of individual and social life which would be unfavourable to religious life. This would mean a situation in which, while God would be theoretically acknowledged, this would make little if any difference to the way in which people really behave. As a consequence Catholicism would be on the one hand the religion of the dominant majority and on the other that of a clear minority.

Data from investigations at least in part confirm the thesis that as in other countries, the moral authority in Poland to some degree has an 'abstract' character. It is acknowledged as a moral institution for the others ('not for me'), but is by no means binding in all spheres of life (e.g. in the sphere of sexual morality).

Under the new socio-political conditions the Catholic Church is incorpo-rated into the life of society in various ways, and many people have specific expectations of its role in maintaining moral values. But the social relativity of the church felt by part of Polish society does not make people conclude that the end of the national church in Poland has come, since the church has not lost its vigour and its importance in social life for the creation of a consensus and the shaping of social awareness. It remains an integral element in the cultural legacy of the nation and an important partner on the stage of public life in Poland. In the meantime, however, estimation of the concrete activity of the church – understood in the context of the results achieved – has become more differentiated and more moderate.

According to the sociologists of religion and pastoral theologians, who do not understand the national church and the community church as opposites, the national church will be renewed especially through the small communities and religious groups which maintain, develop and deepen religious life within the main church. Their activity is important for the future and continuation of the national church – regardless of whether the number of conscious Catholics doubles or triples. The activity of the whole church will be important in warning Poles against spiritual impoverishment, the temptations of a secularization of life and practical nihilism, and in protecting them from it. With insignificant losses, the national church could change and in a sense be strengthened. Perhaps, however, the mass participation of Catholics in religious practices might decline somewhat.

The church in Poland wil not be able to maintain its dominant position on the contemporary ideological market in its previous form, and some forms of thought and action will clearly differ from the religious and church sphere. We are to assume that the processes of a 'creeping' secularization in the twenty-first century will appear in a similar (but not identical) way to those in the highly-developed pluralistic societies. The processes of secularization will be energetically supported by other factors. They are often initiated by those which were at work in the time of real socialism. Thus religion is threatened not only by the social and cultural changes that are taking place, but also by different kinds of ideological initiatives.

Here we must reckon that in the near future, alongside the deepening and strengthening of faith (determined Christians) and alongside the ongoing traditional faith, other attitudes towards religion and church will clearly increase: deliberate selectivity (selective Catholics), individual religion ('religion without the church') and a religious and moral indifferentism. At the beginning of the 1990s it could be observed that people liberated from the control of the Communist system in fact felt free almost to the point of a new lack of freedom. This freedom, including the freedom of faith, is not so much connected with a particular ideological attitude or philosophy as with a quite ordinary laziness in life, with difficult living conditions or even with so-called postmodernity. These people have at most extremely fleeting and superficial religious experiences and most of their religious convictions are based on the tradition handed down by society. Religion too is not a reality which could not be put in doubt.

We must also reckon with an increase in the number of Catholics who have fallen out with the church for political, social or moral reasons. They remain remote from the church because they and their life-style do not fit in with the norms of church law and the moral teaching of the church. This kind of indifference to the church or religion begins with modes of behaviour which are incompatible with Christian norms; it becomes deeper as moral principles are put in question, and only after that affects the sphere of faith and the fundamental content of faith.

Another source of attitudes which are distanced from religion and church is the criticism of the church as an institution, partly formulated and partly arising spontaneously 'from below'; this produces a specific climate of anti-clericalism. This anticlericalism is sometimes stirred up by people who in the 1980s claimed the church as a refuge for national culture. These people have either used the church as an instrument from the beginning or have been disillusioned in the course of their contact with the church and the hierarchy of values which it represents. The anticlericalism is also a side-effect of the autocratic style of leadership in the parishes which is still wide-spread in Polish pastoral care.

This could lead to the church in future becoming less monocentric and turning into a church which is socially and culturally polycentric. Such a course will be favoured by the development of society from modernity to postmodernity, if we understand the problem of the social conditions in which religion and the church function in their two versions, i.e. as variants of opportunities and variants of fears. In that case, at present both possibilities are equally probable. In a process of transition full of opportunities and dangers a completely clear answer would simplify the situation. Even if there is no reason for alarm, nevertheless the social and religious reality does not give any reason for exaggerated optimism, but calls for a deepened evangelization. From another perspective that means that religion and the church must seek a new identity in a constant process under the changing social and cultural conditions.

III. New challenges to pastoral work

The new needs call for an adequate reaction from the church, one which recognizes not only the dangers of a democratic pluralist society but also the possibilities in this society of realizing good and reflecting on new opportunities for proclaiming the gospel. In the rapidly changing society of Poland the evangelizing presence of the church is ever more necessary, indispensable and decisive; its field of activity will in a sense extend further. For there is by no means a sociological or historical necessity for public life in our country to be dominated by a civil bourgeois ideology with indeterminate religious content, or even no such content at all.

Pastoral activity must link up with people's real situation, which is marked by an enormous striving for freedom and by orientation on the affairs of 'this world'. The collective consciousness of Poles is largely dominated by feelings of frustration, of impotence, of passivity, of hopelessness and a retreat into the private sphere. A life only for today, dissatisfaction, apathy, wariness and a lack of orientation towards one's own future as it were darken hope and enthusiasm. To people at a loss, who are convinced of their solitude and have no influence on what is going on around them, who are disillusioned by the functioning of democracy and the social costs of the process of transformation, religion offers no permanent support but only temporary refuge. What is needed is a multi-dimensional way of overcoming the specific anomie in which Polish society has been trapped for many years. Here the church can be only one of many basic structures for social support.

It would be wrong to see the church only as a power which resists the modernization of society. Rather, under the conditions of the gradual construction of democracy after the attainment of freedom, it seeks to help believers to exploit the sphere of freedom and the possibilities of progress in the best possible way, i.e. in a way which does justice to the moral demands. However, the adaptation of the church to modernity and the preferences of so-called modern man come up against limits which must not be exceeded, because this would contradict its mission of evangelization. But it can attempt to recognize the 'holy' in modern culture, i.e. its leading values as they generally accord with the gospel, and present the gospel as a help in reshaping these values.

Three alternative scenarios for the development of religion and the church in the conditions of progressive modernization are discussed in sociology: (a) turning to the past (traditionalism) and resistance to modernity; (b) assimilation to the new social situation through innovation and a change in the religious tradition; (c) overtaking modernity by exploiting its weak points (K.Gabriel).

The starting point of the first scenario is that in some respects the past was better than the present and the future which is coming into view. It is characterized by reserve and restraint, indeed even by opposition to the changes which are taking place with progressive modernization. Religion and the church are not to subject themselves to the influence of society as it modernizes itself, but with the help of traditional forms of pastoral work are to strive to maintain the boundaries between church and society.

The second model presupposes an openness of the church to modernity, collaboration with developing modernity and the attempt to root religion in 'little life-worlds' as the typical forms of postmodern society. That means a weakening of the organized forms of religion in favour of new social forms which are free from the control of church institutions. One symptom of this new religion which has already manifested itself is a form of religion which is distanced from the church; it has the characteristics of an faith which has been experienced, even if these are perhaps remote from the formal faith of the church. This 'liberated' religion still at least needs the support of the church, but is no longer controlled by it. To come to terms with modernity means to accept secularization as a phenomenon which is inseparable from modernization, bound up with the attempt to fulfil the expectations of modern society, which is quite neutral to the 'saints'.

The third model is based on the possibility of reacting swiftly to the development of modern society, of perceiving its imperfections, disappointed hopes, shattered value systems and the contradictions and dilemmas of its development and of creating new forms of social and religious life which meet people's needs ('the great leap forward'). This is a matter of the church being consistently open to the new conditions in which people live in the societies which are being modernized. The starting point for this model – at least indirectly – is that the modern world is characterized not only by 'worldliness' but also by a hunger for salvation and transcendence.

IV. The church's new power of integration

Under the conditions of modernity the church can gain new powers of integration. The postmodernity which has come into being as a result of the crisis offers opportunities for a renewal, and also for a religious renewal. The individualization of human beings, their isolation from others, the way in which many humanistic values are being thrown overboard – these and other weaknesses of modern society offer opportunities for to some degree 'leaping over' modernity. Postmodernity represents not so much a proposal of new contents and new values as the implication of an awareness that modernity has its limits and is based on myths. At present the church is declaring an open standpoint which depends on the conditions but as a whole is benevolent towards the changes in civilization and the process of modernization.

With reference to Polish society, the first model represents the temptation to maintain the national church in its present form and restore the church as an institution for the future which as far as possible is unchanged. By contrast, the second and third models start from a modification of the national church and its adaptation to the new conditions of the pluralistic society, to as to keep up with modernity. Among other things that means a recognition of the manifold forms of religious commitment and a service of the church to people who live their faith in freedom.

The pluralism associated with a diversity of competing value systems existing side by side and with the same rights represents an almost unlimited openness and axiological uncertainty, i.e. such a possibility of choice that in extreme cases it can even lead to the denial of fundamental values and values which are regarded as valid, to the point of sheer arbitrariness. An ethic which is dependent only on human beings must constantly undergo new modifications and reshapings. In the conditions of the moral relativism which is spreading, the church finds it increasingly difficult to permeate the culture of societies in such a way that the message of the gospel becomes the basis of thought and the source of the most important principles of life, criteria of judgment and norms of behaviour. Perhaps in the future it will have to refer more often to the morality of love and forgiveness than to the morality of commands and prohibitions, and also more often use positive and affirmative language in place of the negative language of punishment. Here we are talking about new and more effective forms of preaching faith and morality, not new and immediate programmatic action, but a deepened evangelization of the world and the church.

The new tasks of the church in Poland are more difficult, and call for a fundamental reorientation in the thought and action of believers. The siege mentality must be overcome. The total rejection of modernity is unacceptable, and an attitude of mistrust and fear is inappropriate. Modernity as a collection of particular characteristics of the time and of human mentality can always be accepted by Christians only in part. They do not submit to the solemnity of the changes brought about by modernity but face them critically and judge them in the light of faith. The conscience of Christians not only represents a realization of their own views and thoughts but also relates to the commandments of the God to whom they are responsible.

Religion is not something passive. Its opportunities for the future do not only depend on social development but also have their own dynamic of development. After the regaining of freedom and sovereignty we are confronted with a new stage in the history of our fatherland, with new tasks and new challenges. The Catholic Church in Poland needs a new evangelization and new evangelistic undertakings (the imperative of evangelization).

The new outward conditions in which the church will be active therefore require modernized methods of pastoral work. Such new forms and species in which the gospel can incarnate itself in cultural and social reality will certainly be rediscovered, so that the foundations for a new lasting synthesis of Christian life can be laid. What is important is the ongoing education and development of mature religious personalities and the testimony of Christians themselves in everyday life, also to those who are remote from the church and often regard it with scepticism or even opposition.

The modern pluralistic society does not destroy religion, but it changes its role in society. For believers this means an incessant call to rediscover the roots of their faith, to spiritual renewal and a testimony to their faith in all social circles and spheres of life in which Christians are present.

Translated by John Bowden

The Marginalization of Christians in Eastern Central Europe

MIKLÓS TOMKA

The differences between the countries of Eastern Central Europe in religion, culture and society are greater than those between the countries and regions of Western Europe. The span between Polish piety and East German and Czech atheism, or between the Slovenian consumer society and the rural social order in Romania is a wide one. Some countries are highly industrialized, modern and secularized. Others have clearly pre-modern and non-pluralistic conditions where traditional faith is plausible and has not become problematic. There are religiously homogeneous and multi-confessional societies. In addition there is a factor deriving from the geography of society and religion which some regard as the most important political demarcation;[1] the region is split into two halves by the dividing line between Western and Eastern Christianity.

In social and cultural terms Eastern Central Europe certainly cannot be regarded as a unity. But the Soviet domination has left behind traces of uniformity. The wounds of the past decades are the same in all the countries formerly dominated by Communism, since the totalitarian system produced common factors which stamp these countries. These include the social change brought about under state control, and also the marginalization of Christians. The latter is partly a function of the former, which is why first of all the question of modernization must be discussed. This provides the framework in which the consequences of religious persecution can be described.

I. The change of the position of Christians in the structure of society

'Communist modernization' was implemented as a process in two stages. First the individual countries took the path of industrialization and urbanization at different speeds. Secondly, precisely because of that, the state could control the advancement of society in different orders of magnitude and link up with specific conditions. In the then German Democratic Republic, in Czechia, in Hungary and Slovenia at the beginning of the Communist era, the development of a middle class was in full swing. This could now be accelerated and channelled in accordance with the notions of the state. In other countries this development lagged behind, and as a result the possibilities of remodelling the state, culture and society remained limited.

A word should also be said about the meaning of some key terms used here. Development and *modernization* denote for us the change from rural to urban life; from settled conditions to geographical mobility; from large families to small families; from organic, neighbourly and family ties to formal and legal ties; from a uniform to a plural social and cultural milieu; from an inherited to an achieved social status and ownership of property; from binding tradition to incessant change. Here the first element is by no means just a value judgment. It is simply that two possible orders of social life are being set side by side and the transition from one to another is being noted.

However, a value judgment cannot be avoided in the case of '*Communist modernization*'. This variety is characterized by two additional features. First, it does not follow the genuine patterns and tendencies of a particular society but is imposed 'from above', i.e. by the Party state, and with violence, in accordance with alien (ideological) notions. Accordingly it has far greater social costs than an autonomous change. Secondly, its compulsory character gets in the way of the regeneration process of society: the spontaneous forming of communities, the origin of sub-cultures and the networks of civil society. Some sociologists call this a 'negative modernization', which is marked to a particularly high degree by the lack of communities and which prevents the crystallization of unitary systems of values and social consensuses, even in more immediate milieus.[2]

In particular in the realization of its social vision, Communism has become an enterprise which is hostile to the individual and the community. It sought to improve the self-directed development of society by patterns which were worked out theoretically. But instead of being able to establish a drawing-board order, it merely broke the freedom of development, destroyed the web of human social life and disseminated the arbitrariness of a lack of order. The result was social anomie and in its framework the dulled *homo sovieticus*, poorly motivated and lacking in allegiance, and with a loose and uncertain relationship to religion, if he had any at all.

Communism wanted to implement the same project everywhere, but did not everywhere have the same opportunities. Where the social and economic change had already been set in motion, the hand of the centralist power was relatively light. Where there were fewer conditions favourable to a rapid industrialization; where the rural economy remained in private hands (i.e. had not been appropriated and/or incorporated into socialist concerns); where the surplus population in the province had not emigrated into the cities and where the old social fabric could be preserved, there was no discontinuity in the change. The differences between the countries are differences of degree. But there are clear connections between the economic structure, social mobility, the degree of pluralism, family structure, the growth of the population and public education, along with religion or de-Christianization. Thus in Eastern Central Europe it is possible to distinguish between on the one hand markedly secularized 'modern' countries and on the other 'pre-modern' countries with a higher degree of traditional religion and church membership.[3]

However, it has to be said tine and again that here it is not just a matter of time-lags. The loss of continuity in the tradition and in the social order is not just to be attributed to the socio-economic change, but also to the forcible imposition of it which rode roughshod over the men and women involved. Therefore it would be wrong to think that the few modern countries of Eastern Central Europe in the future simply had to catch up with their 'delay' – in terms of de-Christianization as well. These countries are now encountering the modern world under freer conditions.

Accordingly they have a better opportunity to keep their cultural identity, tradition and even religion than the victims of a successful 'Communist modernization'. However, this perspective does not alter the fact that the more strongly religious countries of Eastern Central Europe (Croatia, Poland, Romania, Slovakia, etc.) are the less modern ones.

The power of Communism arose predominantly from a twofold political possibility – and was backed by the Soviet army. It could annihilate morally and also physically the old middle and upper classes, and develop the new political class that it wanted. In the modern countries there was more than a simple seizure of power. Here the change in the structural composition of society drew the whole of society into its maelstrom. The channels and sluices of growing upward mobility could thus be kept under state control.

Many people attempted to resist the prescriptions of the state. The transformation of ideological notions into social practice could succeed only to a limited degree. But it cannot be denied that the state could make conditions in centralized state socialism: for admission to study and to certain professions, for any advancement, for achieving a higher income, in some periods even for entry into the cities. The condition was ideological reliability, which formally meant membership of the Communist Party or one of the satellite organizations. The statutes of the Communist Party explicitly called for the renunciation of any religion. Less pressure could be put on those who had no aspirations to higher things. By contrast those who wanted advancement were pressurized. It has to be said once again: quite a few succeeded in slipping through the net of state control. But from a statistical perspective the selection functioned successfully. The more hurdles a person had to get over in social advancement, the less was the probability that he or she could preserve their non-conformist identity in the face of the Party state. The higher one looks in the social hierarchy of the countries of Eastern Central Europe, the fewer is the number of Christians. Belief tended to be limited to the lower levels of society.

Communism structurally reinforced the link between religionlessness and higher status.[4] Higher education, professional experience in positions of leadership, the relationships in the networks of the upper classes, or quite simply a better house and the possession of more modern domestic equipment (or the lack of all this), are facts which determine social status and the possibilities of having a say in society over and above any political change. It is a misunderstanding merely to speak of 'roped parties' which preserve their influence even after the change. Rather, it is the case that a social order which has been very deliberately forged over forty or more years can be loosened only slowly, even if it has come into being against the efforts of the majority of the population. Those who have attained a higher position under whatever conditions are now attempting to keep their places. The rising generation even regards its innate status as legitimate and unproblematic. By contrast, those who were robbed and de-classed by the state under Communism or those who in past decades were barred from rising higher can change their situation only in harsh competition within an established order.

The social framework for Christians and the churches in Eastern Central Europe has thus already been provided. Christian faith is present and alive above all in less modern countries and in the more traditional and lower strata. Sometimes Christians and the church can even feel marginalized.

II. Two concomitant phenomena: traditionalism and anxiety about contact

The decades of church persecution have left behind a heavy burden. This consists in the fact that traditionalism has become rigid. Communism used all its weapons against religion. The Christians successfully defended themselves. They preserved their tradition and handed it on. No more and no less.

To begin with, Communism hoped to be able to exterminate God and religion. Soon it had to recognize that it had gone too far: it had to change its policy. From this point on, the Party state did all that it could to shut off faith and the Christians from the public, to constrict the sphere of religion, to isolate the church, and to prevent public witness to Christianity. But at the same time it also sought to exploit the churches for its own purposes.

In the church, both efforts by the state have provoked the same reaction: resistance to all interference and a tendency towards separation. The state wanted to remove faith from 'its' world. The churches withdrew from this world of oppression, violence and apostasy, and attempted to keep their faithful out of it. The state declared the denial of religion a condition of social advancement. That brought the danger that unconsidered experimentation would succumb to the countless seductions and pressures. Thus the church advised against it and used pressure against the temptation to engage in such games. By contrast, the state thought it important to exclude from the visible life of the church people involved in education or in positions of leadership. The religious community began to suspect and avoid those Christians who held offices which the state generally reserved for non-believers. It felt that such people could not be wholly trustworthy; certainly they must have made some concessions to attain their positions.

This strategy of building bulkheads did not just develop overnight. It took a while for the view to be established in the church that totalitarian systems offered almost no way for practising Christians to achieve social advancement. (Almost none! Nowhere were the ways ever completely blocked. Everywhere there were secret paths, for example through the arts or through sporting successes, perhaps in the natural sciences, but all this required quite special achievements.) But the moment that – in addition to state discrimination – the isolation of the church began, people found countless arguments to justify it. In fact the further the retreat from the public sphere, the more removed from it people felt.

This demarcation from the evil world is not a new idea. The church authorities knew this strategy very well from the confrontation between the world church and rising liberalism in the second half of the nineteenth century and the beginning of the twentieth. At that time, in many countries the church attempted to establish and maintain a 'counter-world' with its own institutions and its own structure of organizations. From a sociological perspective this attempt was not uninteresting. It was able to remedy the lack of education among Catholics and generally secure their emancipation. However, under Communism the conditions were rather different. To begin with, the social isolation of Christians was only to a degree self-chosen: it was forced on them. But once it was affirmed, the Christian community lost any sense of the seismic tremors in society. That is the tragedy of the churches of Eastern Central Europe. They have lost contact with society and history. And they are not blameless here.

In the end there was a cultural delay both in the development of a separate society and also – even more markedly – in connection with the changes in the world church. This delay took its revenge at three levels. The church finds it very difficult to discover the right tone to use towards youth. It finds it almost impossible to join in the most topical questions of society, science and culture. Therefore it has an additionally disturbed relationship to the cultural elite. Finally, it does not understand the (post)modernity into which Eastern Central Europe is slithering. This position is largely predestined as a result of its former behaviour. In addition, the preservation of a backward-looking conservatism is further strengthened socially by the fact that the vast majority of Christians in Eastern Europe who are loyal to the church – despite a marked change in the past one or two decades – are to be found in the premodern countries and in the older, rural, less educated and lower strata of society.

This marginal position, along with the way in which the church lags behind developments, produces everyday conflicts which demonstrate the church's lack of ability in the social interplay of forces. While the clashes in the competitiveness of pluralism are often in fact harsh, they are basically normal phenomena. After the experiences of decades of persecution, though, the church usually reads them in a completely different way. Social and cultural traditionalism continues to regard the hegemony of religion and the church – with a uniform moral order which extends through society and with very close friendly relations between state and church – as the norm. If this does not exist or is even rejected in post-Communist society, the cause of this must, it is thought, be hostility to religion. Conflicts of interest and occasional collisions are interpreted as persecution of the church. Variety of opinion (particularly within the church) is rejected as betrayal of the truth. Social groups which pursue aims which indisputably diverge from those of the church or run contrary to them, or which enter into opposition to the church, are set up by shady characters.

The church in Eastern Central Europe has not yet been able to overcome its suffering; it has not yet got rid of a persecution complex. It would be wrong to regard this as only a sickness or even as a delusion. The experience of current 'persecution' has quite tangible foundations, even if some of them are interpreted wrongly. In part they are to be sought in the tensions of a pluralism which is used very roughly, and in part they attest the inferior social status of Christians.

III. The new starting point for faith and Christians

The churches have withstood the test of persecution, but they have emerged from it diminished, impoverished and humiliated. Most countries of Eastern Central Europe are now experiencing a religious renewal. That gives reason for optimism. But it does not alter the fact that in many countries Christians have become a minority and that in almost all the former Communist states they are in a disadvantaged social position. Those are the facts. The question is what message this fate has for Christians.

The time of persecution and the losses can be interpreted as a visitation, as a punishment from God, as trials which have to be withstood. They can be interpreted as only negative experiences which impose no obligations on a person other than to persist in the good. But it makes sense to dig a little deeper. Even if one has a punitive God in view, one should ask about the occasion for the punishment. Is it simply enough to talk of 'our sins' or has the nature of the punishment something to do with the special character of the sins? Is not the church of God being called to account for its un-Christian domination, for its rejection of some human rights, for its brother-hood with the secular power, for its trust in its institutions and its cultural power? But God is not in the first place the penal judge, but the creator and loving Father who cares for his creatures. God's actions towards us are not primarily punishments, but pointers to something better. Surprising consequences can be drawn from this conviction.

Christians have become a minority which is discriminated against and even now is still at a disadvantage. Christians are less educated, in lower positions and less prosperous than average in society. They cannot testify to being Christians through a higher knowledge, through social influence or through their economic power. Their social attitude reminds them that they cannot do any of this. Perhaps they had to experience such humiliation to see that the means of this world do not bring any additional strength to Christian discipleship. The Christians of Eastern Central Europe now face the challenge of seeking their future not in restoring their church organizations and their former positions of power, but in entrusting themselves to Christ alone.

However, in the Communist period the church acquired a valuable treasure. Lay Christians met in communities and recognized their responsibility for one another, for the church and for the world. They stood up for their convictions and were respected for this by their fellow citizens. Through them (and not through the priests, far less through the bishops) the church in many places gained a respect which perhaps it never had before. To say this is not to criticize the clergy. It is merely to quote the statement that there are places and conditions in which the church can be present, effective, the salt of the earth, only through the laity.[5] The modern pluralistic world in general seems to reflect such a situation. Important though the reappearance of the ministry, organization and institutions of the church may be, in Eastern Central Europe it has beyond doubt damaged the social reputation of Christianity. The people of God now faces the question how lay commitment can be maintained and fostered at a time in which the priestly leadership structure of the church is being reconstructed.

IV. Challenges to planning and guidance in the church

Relevant signs of the time for Eastern Central Europe can be found both in the period of Communism and in the time after the change. The church has been painfully reminded of its secularization and of the fact that it previously allied itself with the great powers of this world. Now it can be grateful for the steps which led it, through the force of Communism, into poverty, insignificance and suffering. Probably in these years it has come closer to its Lord than it was before.

The new situation brought new challenges. The hunger for religion and freedom of opinion define the present responsibility in just as new a way as the growing social distress and the desire for social activity on the part of the church. By contrast, the minority situation of believers, their tendency towards conservatism and the continuing isolation of the church from society are limiting factors. They damage the personal development of Christians and also the presence and effectiveness of the church. Four priorities arise out of the tension between tasks and capacity, which are more important than any plan for restoring the church's organization.

1. *Responsibility of the laity*

Among other things the social marginalization causes passivity and immaturity. These must be overcome. The basic question in really becoming a Christian, which is also a question about the survival of the church on the threshold to (post)modernity, is how the personal responsibility of the laity can be aroused and incorporated into the actions and the decisions of the church. If this is to happen, lay people must be taken seriously, addressed, prepared, entrusted with tasks, given responsibility and authority, and not least be brought together and kept together in communities.

However, no one can relieve the priests and bishops of their central role in fulfilling these tasks. Therefore perhaps the first step is to convince and retrain the clergy. The priests have not been prepared for such a giant task. The training of priests always takes place in a separate sphere, out of contact with the world and the Christian communities. The past decades have further heightened the isolation of the priests. Often too they have no free time. So first perhaps it must be made clear that nothing may come before the creation of an active community of believers. The priest is called to be a shepherd, to go after the sheep which have gone astray, to restore community. The sacraments are sacraments for the community of believers (and not for the masses). The fostering of active and mature communities is the alpha and the omega of the priestly ministry. Looking after a Christian community which is conscious of its responsibilities may claim all the reserves of a priest, but it multiplies his forces. The education of colleagues is not time wasted, but the seed which will soon bear fruit.

2. *Christian education*

The incorporation of the laity has a special component in Eastern Central Europe. Some of the most committed laity have become unduly used to being loners, or to being in their own little encapsulated communities. They have to be 'tamed', reconciled with the clergy, brought into the greater unity of the church. The time for partisanship is over. They must also see that. But conversely, the solidarity and freedom to which these people had previously been accustomed must also be realized within the church. And the clergy must recognize the achievements of these lay people, made with great sacrifice, rather than mistrusting them. In most countries of Eastern Central

Europe it was incomparably easier to be a priest than to be an active Catholic in an academic profession. A church which has become a minority cannot afford the luxury of simply discarding its most valuable witnesses from previous decades.

The second priority is the extension and qualitative improvement of Christian education. Today religion is not a fit conversation partner for culture and science; and the reasons for this do not lie solely in Communism. Every bishop has the right to appoint a pastor with a doctorate to a chair in theology. But no academic achievements, publications, or involvement in scholarly life are expected of professors. They often have no time for this alongside their pastoral activity. They find it difficult to keep up with their subject because of a lack of literature and of professional exchanges. However, their episcopal nomination protects them from any competition. But the bishops themselves often have neither qualifications nor interest in exercising control over what goes on in colleges. Thus theology goes to the dogs.

Laity are admitted to chairs in theological faculties only in the rarest exceptions. The church regards the study of theology and disciplines related to religion in state faculties with mistrust and makes them difficult to engage in. Certainly Christian education and lay training are usually affirmed, but no one takes responsibility for them. So far it has been left to chance and to the initiative of individual Christians whether Christianity is taught and represented with the quality needed for proper dialogue. In most countries in Eastern and Central Europe such attempts are not encouraged by the church, and only beginnings have been made by the world church, e.g. through Renovabis and KAAD in Germany. By contrast, in the liberal sphere countless grants have been made to promote this. The militant liberal billionaire George Soros even maintains his own universities in Budapest and Warsaw, and sends students to them from all over the former Communist region at his own expense.

If the church wants to break through its cultural marginalization, it will have to turn to the educational sector. The magnitude of this task makes it obvious that here the hierarchy is being addressed. Christian academic education is the key to a dialogue with educationalists, with scientists and with the youth who are studying. Progress in this direction collides with traditionalism. However, the capacity of Christian culture for dialogue requires the renunciation of any integralism. But this step will not be taken everywhere.

3. Dialogue with society

In a first attempt after the change, the churches seem to have hoped for an improvement of their situation through state treaties and legal regulations. This approach may have been justified in so far as the blatant Communist violations of the law had to be repaired. In the process of the formation of a new constitution, religion and the church also had to be given a place in the order and negotiated with. But the church's claims brought the non-believers and the supporters of the abdicated order to the barricades. The church was again regarded by some people as a great power, even as an enemy. It was a pity that we had to pay for the normalization of the legal and organizational position of the church by alienating a large part of the population of Eastern Central Europe from it. A third priority of the period after the change therefore consisted in reviving the dialogue with society. Such a relationship cannot be filled with life solely by church officials. The same priority also applies to the development of Christian communities and organizations, i.e. to the structure of the church as part of a secular civic society and a counter to it.[6] (It should be mentioned in passing that this affects the way in which the collaboration is arranged and ministries and responsibilities in the church.)

4. Grappling with modernization

A fourth priority above all applies to the less modernized countries. Only now do these countries face a comprehensive social differentiation and secularization, because for a long time they could avoid a socio-economic change and greater mobility and maintain their traditional culture. They gained valuable time. However, they do not have a special way round modernity. If the churches of these countries learn from the experiences of the more modern societies, they will be able to lessen the decline in religion which takes place in the process of the loss of tradition. They must grapple with the potential consequences of modernization, and in their development must not lag too far behind the bulk of society. That is an almost impossible demand, considering the relative marginality of the Christians in these lands also. Here the international character of the church can be some help. But first of all the mutual reservations must be demolished. Here at any rate is an opportunity for the modern countries of Eastern Central Europe to be responsible for the less modern countries and also for the church of the West to be responsible for the churches of the Eastern countries – it is a responsibility for one another, for the whole church of Christ.

We are faced with the marginality of the Christian people, of the church of Eastern Central Europe. We must accept this in order to deal with it, and we must try to overcome it in order to break through the barriers which are imposed on the mission of the church. Both accepting and overcoming these barriers calls for superhuman strength. It would be wrong if the church, the bishops and Christians were primarily to rely on their own wisdom and capacities. They should build on the One who has promised that he will not forsake his church. With this confidence the church can venture steps which it could never take all on its own. The creative overcoming of the situation of minorities calls for a bold faith.

Translated by John Bowden

Notes

1. Samuel P. Huntington, *The Clash of Civilizations*, New York 1996.
2. Elemér Hankiss, *East European Alternatives*, Oxford 1990.
3. Miklós Tomka and Paul M.Zulehner, *Religion im gesellschäftlichen Kontext Ost(Mittel) Europas*, Ostfildern 2000.
4. There is statistical and sociological evidence in Detlef Poillack, Irena Borowik and Wolfgang Jagodzinski (eds), *Religiöser Wandel in den postkommunistichen Länder Ost- und Mitteleuropas*, Würzburg 1998; Tomka and Zulehner, *Religion in gesellschäftlicher Kontext* (n.3); ibid., *Religion in den Reformlander Ost(Mittel) Europas*, Ostfildern 1999; Miklós Tomka et al., *Religion und Kirchen in Ost(Mittel) Europa: I. Ungarn, Litauen, Slowenien*, Ostfildern 2000.
5. *Lumen Gentium*, 33.
6. José Casanova, *Public Religions in the Modern World*, Chicago and London 1994.

The Change in the Religious Situation in the Eyes of Non-Believers

MARKO KERŠEVAN

My remarks are conditioned by my experiences in Slovenia, a country which was certainly not a standard Communist country; it was the most Western of the Communist countries, and not just in the geographical sense. Therefore here the possibilities and limitations of the church and the Christian religion in such systems manifest themselves in a specific way.[1]

I. The church and religion in the socialist system

Socialism did not fall from heaven, nor did it come from hell. As an ideology and a theory it came into being in the nineteenth century as the attempt at an answer to the crises and conflicts of the rising modern capitalist world in what were then by far the most developed industrial nations. It triumphed politically in capitalist undeveloped Russia and the countries of Central and South Eastern Europe, countries which (according to Lenin) were the weakest European members of world capitalism. It established itself there in the form of 'real socialism'. It triumphed during the two decisive crises of this world, in the time of two world wars and their consequences. It also triumphed by offering promises of a way out of a world which had caused such catastrophes and millions of victims. It triumphed – still at that time – in the radical version of a minority, i.e. in the Communist version.

As a theory and an ideology Socialism regarded itself as the vehicle and realization of bourgeois, modern achievements, the values of freedom, equality and brotherhood, and of modern individualism; after all, 'the free development of each is the condition for the free development of all' is the aim of the Communist Manifesto of 1848.[2] In its radical versions, at the same time it turned against the basic principles of the modern world: the market economy, formal democracy and the economic and social inequalities which arose out of these; here it also found support in the values of the Christian gospel. Such an ambivalent relationship with the modern world, which was already rooted in the theory of results, was reinforced in the later development, in theory and even more in practice. On the one hand in the traditionalist Eastern societies socialism appeared as the vehicle of modern Western values: from technological progress and industrialization to – at least in its rhetoric – equal rights for women, for example in women being given the vote. On the other hand the Eastern traditions and conditions within which it was effective further reinforced its hostile orientation towards modernity (statism, the omnipotent state, collectivism, the leader cult, etc.). Or, seen from another perspective: in its striving for greater equality it suspended freedom and at the same time created new, politically conditioned inequalities. Even if it satisfied some basic existential needs of the people, above all the working classes, relatively successfully (full employment, social welfare and insurance for sickness and old age, opportunities of education, basic medical care), at the same time it deprived the (potentially) dynamic educated classes of motive and turned them against themselves.

This ambivalent attitude of Communist socialism to the processes of modernization in the conditions of Eastern Europe needs to be noted in an investigation of the ambivalent consequences of its collapse in these societies – and also in respect of the position of religion and the church.[3]

Eastern Communism also saw itself as a vehicle and realization of progressive Western bourgeois principles in relations with religion and the church. First came the principle of a consistent separation of church and state. But here this separation was accompanied by two characteristics alien to modernity: a totalitarian view of the competence of the state and its *de facto* ideological partisanship. The one-party state realized the programme and the guidelines of the Party; this also included the 'ideological battle against religion', 'the dying out of religion', and the like. Of course the church already stood in the way of the Party and the one-party state simply as an actual and potential ideological and organizational rival.

However, it must be noted that the difference in system between 'state' and 'party' nevertheless remained. Neither the constitution nor the laws contained regulations which explicitly discriminated against believers; the laws relating to the religious communities as a rule protected the freedom of confession of faith and the practice of religion within the narrow framework mentioned above, even if these were viewed differently in the different countries: conditions in Poland or in Slovenia were not like those in the Soviet Union or in Czechoslovakia. The exclusion of active believers from certain areas of the state apparatus or from the higher and highest levels of the professional or political hierarchy took an informal course, and certainly the Party had a great influence, if not a monopoly, on personal politics in all areas. As a rule membership of the Communist Party was incompatible with profession of a religion or membership of a church.

Yet another characteristic of the Yugoslav system or its ideology should not be overlooked: the principle of respect for the 'masses', above all the masses of workers, the 'will of the people'. Given the declared and ideologically necessary respect for the will and feeling of the masses, for better or for worse, one could not simply leave aside the feelings of these masses about religious belief. That found expression in the explicit indication that as a system or as a movement socialism was not anti-religious but – regardless of its attitude to religion – was concerned for the good of all citizens and especially the workers. Hence the repeated reckonings within the Party with 'sectarians' who put the 'struggle with religion' first or waged the struggle in such a way that 'feelings about faith' were violated and 'honest believers' were alienated from the Party and from socialism. This is also the source of a politically differentiated attitude towards religion and church, for example the rule that while the activity of the masses, the working classes and the peasant classes, in the church and religion are to be respected, at the same time the active believers in certain strata of the intelligentsia must be controlled and discriminated against. Present-day surveys of public opinion reflect this situation very well: in most countries the majority of the population who are not very old are of the view that belief and the church were not always persecuted in the time of Communism; they themselves or their acquaintances were not the victims of discrimination.[4]

II. Ways and developments after the change

After the collapse of the Communist system the social situation of religion and the church can develop in two possible directions. The first maintains the principle of the separation of state and church; here the state or public institutions now behave in a neutral way and do not take sides with the atheistic ideology as once they did. At the same time the modern state now sets itself limits. It guarantees civil society, and within this society also guarantees wise scope for the activity of the churches and faith communities. The second forms a privileged alliance between the state (which formally can be neutral, or can be separated from the faith communities) and the 'national' church. But at the same time it appropriates these – at least symbolically – public or state institutions, which, while excluding or compelling no one, on the basis of symbols of faith, rituals or the substance of faith (one thinks of instruction about a particular religion in schools) at least symbolically are not open to all to the same degree.

In this context let us now look at some developments or dilemmas in connection with the situation of religion and the church.

1. A new religious departure?

The growth of religion attested by many indicators since as early as the end of the 1970s, especially in Hungary and Slovenia, can be explained by several interlinked hypotheses:

1. The secularized collective Communist eschatology of the realization of a 'new society' had vanished to the level of rhetoric in late real socialism. The dominant ideology became the really conservative ideology of maintaining the status quo and its advantage. The decline of the collectivist eschatology stimulated the search for an individualized identity and a corresponding sense of meaning. That led to the revival of old national identities. Both these have reactualized the potential of the church and religion in the conditions of Central and Eastern Europe.
2. A critical distancing from the system led to identification with institutions outside the system and institutions which were against the system; the churches were understood as such institutions.
3. In fact the conservative ideology of late real socialism no longer found itself on an unavoidable collision course with the Christian religion, but merely on a colllision course with a particular mode of its existence and action, i.e. above all the Catholic Church. A more neutral attitude of the official ideology to religion released the desire, above all in the middle classes (for example among bureaucrats, who usually are the most conformists), to profess religion.
4. After the collapse of the socialist systems and in the time of the change, greater uncertainty, risk and also hopelessness in broad strata contributed to as increased attractiveness of religious questions and religious answers. One thing should not be overlooked: according to surveys in recent years, most people in the Reform countries of Eastern Europe judged the time before 1989 to be better and happier,[5] presumably as a time of greater certainty, solidarity and firmer values.

2. The revival of public church activity

Investigations carried on in before 1990 in Slovenia showed an interesting difference: sensitivity and a critical attitude towards the then discrimination against believers was widespread. At the same time people felt that the churches had sufficient freedom for their activities. It seems that a large proportion even of Catholic believers accepted the limitation of the church to sacramental worship, parish catechesis and pastoral work in the private sphere which was imposed by the system. This was seen as a concentration of the church on its right and essential task, whereas in the pre-Communist era it had discredited itself to a large degree by its wider public actions as a politically and culturally conservative institution striving for domination. In Slovenia it actually contributed to division and bloody conflicts even among believers precisely by such behaviour, by its political ambitions and its incompetence. Hence the understandable anxiety that a revival of the public and political role of the church could again revive and deepen the polarization which developed at that time. Of course the Communists had their own reasons and calculations in excluding the church from public political life, but the support which they received also arose from the negative experiences of a church which had been too strongly politicized and clericalized.

3. Increase in church institutions

The church institutions in the sphere of education, in the social sphere, in health care and in charitable work need to be recognized, and in times when there was a lack of such institutions they were welcomed. In the pre-Communist period the Catholic Church was also active and successful in these spheres, in Slovenia as elsewhere in Central Europe. The Communist power deprived the church of all such institutions and similarly of the means of maintaining them. But it also took the tasks of these institutions and welfare upon itself; as a rule its care was by no means worse than that of the church previously. Given the relative poverty and backward economy almost everywhere, the concern of the real-socialist systems for educational, health and social institutions was generally their strength. In view of the denationalization that is taking place or the founding of new institutions in this sphere by the church, people justifiably ask why these are necessary now in place of the former public institutions – or in parallel to them. The answer then emerges that here the church is pursuing quite partisan, so to speak selfish, interests, above all when it strives to act with the aid of public funding. Should it not rather be making a contribution towards seeing that the neutral public and communal institutions function well? Should it not expand their activity and supplement these with its special religious and pastoral work? Why should the Catholic population in particular have separate education and be looked after in Catholic kindergartens, schools, boarding schools, hospitals, and social and recreational institutions? Why in the name of pluralism and freedom must in fact a dualism be introduced between Catholic and public institutions (the latter now being neutral), above all if there is no lack of the latter and the Catholics expect to be financed from the same sources?

4. Denationalization and restitution

In Slovenia and other countries many believers, and of course those who did not belong to the church, were amazed at the uncompromising insistence by the church on a denationalization and restoration of all the former church property which had been 'stolen' from the church. The uncompromising insistence of the church on its claim to 'make good the injustice', the insistence on its own rights and the lack of readiness to listen to counter-arguments, or at least to recognize the possibly good will of those who advanced them – all this gave the impression that the church was a selfish alliance of interests. It seemed to confirm the well known evaluation in Marx's Preface to *Das Kapital* that the – Anglican – church would rather do without thirty-eight of the Thirty-Nine articles than without a thirty-ninth of its income. The argument that this property was now needed for wider activity for the benefit of all (Catholics) is not convincing enough, as we saw. Certainly, for example in Slovenia, the opposition has used various political and legal tricks to thwart the restoration of property, but one does not expect the same moral and unselfish attitude from the institutions concerned as one does from the church. The insistence on the restoration of estates to natural woodland, the intensive development of its own activities (banking), the rejection or belittling of proposals for a voluntary church tax on the Spanish or Italian model – all this gives the impression of the behaviour of a caste which is striving for (financial) independence both from the state and from believers, as it trusts neither the one nor the others.

III. Links between the church and politics

Certainly the church and the democratic societies take it for granted that the churches should also have a presence in politics. But the question arises what the right mode of such a presence is in a particular land and in specific conditions. For Reform countries with similar historical experiences to Slovenia, it is certainly not right if the church emerges in an indissoluble alliance with one of two political blocks, regardless of whether it is active here as a motive force or as a supporter). Nor can it be right for the church always to take the side which in a given political setting gives it more rights and/or a more rapid implementation of these rights. With such conduct and such a self-image its fundamental moral and religious role loses all credibility. Here it cannot argue that the 'others', the opposite side, are the same or even worse. The church must find political themes which clearly indicate that it is not a prisoner (or leading co-founder) of the existing party-political grouping; it must not be afraid of going against the tide.

It would be to the benefit of all if the Catholic Church could grow out of an exclusively polemic attitude which understands a rejection of church demands and arguments (on the questions mentioned above) merely as a 'hate campaign' by the 'old' or even 'hellish powers' against the church. It would be to the benefit of all if – especially in societies like that of Slovenia, which are polarized into Catholics and non-Catholics – the church clearly expressed by its action that it was not concerned with a new Reconquista or Counter-Reformation but needed to ensure that its previous contribution was acknowledged and that there were the possibilities of a wider positive contribution to a more human and more fulfilled social life in the common sphere. Here it must for its part recognize and make possible such a contribution from the other, the non-Catholic side: from the Protestants to the socialists, Communists, liberals, atheists and so on. Such a mutual recognition of achievements and values does not exclude criticism and polemic; on the contrary it creates a permanent and firm basis for them. But this criticism is correct and productive only when one compares one's own principles and ideals with the principles and ideals of others; if one compares actions with actions, results with results, and also connections between the principles, goals and actions of each side. It is not a matter of comparing our exalted ideals with the evil deeds of others or our prominent personalities and their achievements with the suspect purposes and goals of others.

Translated by John Bowden

Notes

1. M. Tomka and P. Zulehner, *Religion in den Reformländern Ost (Mittel) Europa*, Ostfildern 1999; D. Pollack, I. Borowik and W. Jagodzinski (eds), *Religiöser Wandel in den postkommunistischen Ländern Ost- und Mitteleuropas*, Würzburg 1998; R. Wuthnow (ed.), *The Encyclopedia of Politics and Religion*, London 1998; E. Nembach (ed.), *Jugend – 2000 Jahre nach Jesus*, Jugend und Religion in Europa II, Frankfurt am Main 1996.

2. Cf. Marx and Engels, *Werke* 4, Berlin 1974, 482.

3. Cf. M. Kerševan, 'Sozialismus', *Evangelisches Kirchenlexikon* 4, Göttingen 1994, 355–62; id., 'L'ambivalence de la révitalisation religieuse dans les sociétés postsocialistes', *Social Compass* 40, 1999, 123–33.

4. Tomka and Zulehner, *Religion in den Reformländern* (n.1), 47, 50.

5. Ibid., 152.

Modes of Religious Education in Slovenia

STANKO GERJOLJ

I. Religious socialization in the family

Throughout the period of Communism, despite intensive attempts to devalue the family, it remained the decisive institution in bringing up children. All surveys of young people indicate that the family, and above all the mother, played a crucial role in the decisions that they made.[1] However, different types of family style developed in such upbringing: some families or parents adopted an educational style like that of the schools; a second type of family came closer to the style of education in the church; and a third, the vast majority of parents, attempted to get along without causing friction with either of these educational institutions. In these families many tasks of upbringing were mostly left to school and church.[2]

At decisive moments, the majority of parents supported education in school. Under Communism people became accustomed to making pragmatic, superficial and short-sighted decisions. They learned to conceal their private lives; from childhood on to lead a double life; and to adapt completely to the pressures and expectations of the public, which had been shaped by the Communist Party and its authorities.[3] Above all this weakened sense of responsibility made people insensitive and superficial; they lost their orientation the moment that the Communist Party had to give up its position of power.[4]

1. Conflicts between the generations and problems of identity

Logically this superficiality and lack of sensitivity in the generations which were educated by the Communists and are now already adults is also having its effect on children and young people. After the revolution many adults have lost their credibility, above all for the young. This has put parents in a difficult position, with which they find it extremely difficult to cope, if they can cope at all. Such circumstances perplex both young people and adults, above all in situations of conflict, and often provoke aggressive behaviour in both generations. Even parents are often challenged and virtually forced to concede that they supported, or at least tolerated, a system which at its core was totalitarian and inhuman.[5] They have to concede that they have sacrificed their lives for something which proved totally lacking in perspective and meaning, the moment that the Communist dictatorship collapsed. This forces them into an identity crisis in which they have to confess that they have as it were lived 'in vain'.

Adults are sensitive to such accusations and powerless to respond to them, since as children of the Communist revolution they were themselves even motivated to despise and to hate anything that did not correspond with Communist-dominated education and with socialism. This had already shaped their attitudes to their own parents when these did not want to go along with Communism. Now they find themselves in a situation in which their children are doing the same thing, but with the difference that the accusations which they face are more realistic and nearer to the truth than those which they once made.

So young people are not apathetic and aggressive because they cannot cope with conflicts, but because they face an apathetic and passive generation of adults with which they can do and achieve whatever they like.[6] Therefore the apathy and aggression of the youth are not to be understood as capitulation to many conflicts but in a certain sense as a lack of experience of being involved in conflicts.

2. Religious education in the family

The 'socialist revolution' which began fifty years ago broke radically with the past. As we saw above, everything that recalled the past had from this moment to be hated and despised. The pressure of having to live in a first beginning, i.e. without any cultural, religious and national history of their own, aroused above all in the young generations the feeling of an absence of history and, connected with that, an uncertainty about life.[7]

When totalitarianism began to totter, it was again predominantly the youth who showed an interest in their predecessors, in the way in which they lived and the stories that they told. They wanted to revive the old traditions and customs and thus bring a bit of the past and history into the present. In some families this set in motion new processes of communication and socialization. However, there are still many families who are rapidly changing their lifestyle in respect of religious behaviour. Many of them feel at home in various church movements and not a few – possibly in order to catch up with what they have neglected – incline to religious fanaticism. Often the con-

Stanko Gerjolj

verts have to face difficulties in the course of the process of integration into the life of the church community, since some traditional members regard them with scepticism and antipathy.

A second category of family remained steadfast and faithful to the church even during Communism. They now feel justified, but their religious life has hardly changed. Under Communism they felt forced into a ghetto situation. Even now they find it difficult to break out of its confines. Parents basically provide a more traditional religious education; they regard changes and renewals with scepticism.

In generally, however, religious socialization in families is declining, at least quantitatively. The media, above all television and the PC, seem to be the main reasons for this. A good 45% of children between the ages of seven and fourteen in Slovenia watch more than three hours of television a day, and more than 65% of families have a computer in the house. The result of this is that while 69.5% of children who attend catechesis pray almost every day,[8] as one would expect there are few families which practise daily prayer. While 17.5% of the total population of Slovenia (in 1991 71.36% of the population) declared themselves to be Catholics, hardly 10% of the generation between thirty and forty-five, the generation which is decisive for religious socialization in the families, pray at all.[9]

II. School and the question of religious instruction

With the first democratic elections, the educational system was exposed to the danger of becoming the victim of a revolution for the second time. Had the spokesmen of the tradition succeeded in changing the schools as the institutional vehicles of education suddenly and in a revolutionary way, i.e. by compulsion, the past would again have been suppressed and the continuity would have been broken.[10] The conviction that the past was bad did not justify deleting it and passing over it; even a bad past remains a reality. If one wants to overcome it, one must first take note of it and reflect on it.

Moreover, the personnel responsible for education had been trained in a strictly Marxist way. Since non-Marxists had virtually no entry into this group, most teachers and professors were happy in their sphere of activity. So any sudden change could have been made only in the way and with the totalitarian means by which the Communists achieved their aims after the Second World War.

So it was not merely out of a sense of impotence but mainly out of theoretical and political conviction that the representatives who inclined towards the tradition opted for the difficult, laborious, above all slow, but democratic way of initiating processes of change in education. It is therefore no wonder that (at least as far as the curriculum is concerned) it has been impossible to achieve virtually anything except the removal of the Communist-ideological subjects from the curriculum.

However, the legal acceptance of private schools may be regarded as a success story for democratization. Ways have already been found for the private schools not just to be tolerated by the state but also to be integrated into the educational system and given financial support.[11] (This applies mainly to four Catholic senior secondary schools.) However, the problematical feature still remains that it is left to the state to withdraw approval for a private school at any time – if it proves that this could threaten the existence of a state school in a geographical region.[12]

1. The question of religious instruction

Only in 1993 were representatives of the church invited to collaborate in a negotiating commission appointed to clarify the presence of religion in school education and the teaching of religion. Once the church had been invited to put forward its own proposals, it opted for 'ethical religious education' conceived of as a compulsory subject. This proposal was not accepted by the government commission.

In this connection there is talk of an 'ideologically neutral' and 'autonomous' school.[13] Behind this, however, despite the theoretical trimmings, there is clearly an effort by politicians with Communist and liberal leanings to continue to use the school as a political means for their own end. The materialistic view which used to be called 'scientific' is now replaced by a world-view which is described as 'neutral and autonomous', from which references of transcendence remain likewise excluded. In this way, above all the ideology of the liberal party which has been in power since 1991 is to be communicated.

The current policy with a 'liberal' stamp has now, for the last three of the nine years of full-time and still uniform school education, introduced the compulsory subject 'knowledge of homeland and ethics'. In parallel to this subject, religious education is to be taught as a non-confessional voluntary subject under the heading 'religions and ethics'; both in respect of the teachers and the content this is to be taught exclusively by state institutions.[14] The church has not accepted this scheme, but has dissociated itself from it.[15]

Once again a scheme characteristic of Communism is in prospect for schools. Here the two subjects relating to ethics, world-view, religion and other existential questions (the compulsory subject 'knowledge of homeland and ethics' and the voluntary subject 'religions and ethics') are to be taught solely under the aegis of the state. That means that the state or the state apparatus assumes the right to be the only institution which determines the values and world-view to be disseminated at school. It must be said that there is a danger here of a form of education conceived of in terms of the state.

By contrast, the church and an increasingly large proportion of the public are supporting a concept of schooling which offers the individual more possibilities of choice. As advocates of a pluralistic and democratic schooling they argue for 'world views' as a voluntary or compulsory subject. Here they are taking a step in the direction of democracy and pluralism. They want to offer not just 'scientific, ideologically neutral or autonomous', uniform and preconceived, interpretations of existential questions, but also alternative answers; they want to make individual decisions possible.[16]

The question of religious instruction has not been solved in Slovenia. Some church representatives and politicians think it a pity that the first democratically elected government led by the Christian Democrats did not introduce religious instruction, if need be by decree. On the other hand, it is appropriate and certainly a great gain that the question has already been discussed for almost ten years. Granted, there is still no solution, but when one does come, it will not have been dictated from above but will have been thoroughly discussed, indeed fought over. One hopes that this will be the basis of a long-term practice which above all will provoke less aggression. According to proposals being discussed at present, the existing parish catechesis could be recognized by the school as a voluntary subject. In discussions so far this proposal has also received most public approval. Pupils who in the last three years of compulsory school education must take at least three of the around forty voluntary subjects on offer, and who in any case attend parish catechesis, could have this recognized as a voluntary subject. Although some questions are open, especially that of finance, as a result of this the quality of catechesis would certainly improve. First, the existing processes of socialization and integration could continue within the church community, and secondly, some catechists would have to receive better training. On the basis of the discussion so far the catechists must be appointed by the church. But they must also meet all the professional requirements for teaching prescribed by the state.

III. Religious socialization in the church

In its specific task of religious education the church regards the school and the family as two educational institutions which supplement and enrich each other. The church of Slovenia is becoming increasingly aware – not without tensions and difficulties – that also in the context of European culture and life it can no longer present itself as the sole mediator of truths and views of life. It must also note that it cannot realize and keep its own identity by putting up the shutters, but above all needs religious socialization and integration into the specific religious communities. The proposal for religious instruction along the lines of catechesis is also to be seen in this context.[17]

In Slovenia, around 63% of pupils between six and fifteen years of age attend parish catechesis. The sacrament of confirmation, which is usually administered between the age of twelve and fifteen, plays an important role here. As the number of those who attend parish catechesis after being confirmed usually sinks drastically, some parishes tend to raise the age of confirmation to sixteen or even eighteen.[18] Barely 8% of young people between the ages of sixteen and twenty-seven take an active part in church parish life, and only 5–6% of the young people of this age attend a youth catechesis.

Thus the church certainly faces many challenges in youth work. In individual cases new perspectives and possibilities are opening up; they relate above all to social, charitable, religious and cultural, educational and sporting activities. On the basis of these forms of influence which extend beyond the liturgy and yet are bound up with faith, the young people who are less burdened with the past can assume a pioneer role in the attempt to break through or creatively to bridge the wall separating private life (including religion) from public life which was erected under Communism. Here the leadership of the Catholic church of Slovenia can rely on a general solidarity of Christians with the clergy. Against this background, and given the experiences of the churches of the West, it is making considerable efforts to bring together all the groups, sections and associations with the local parishes and the official church. But this will not relieve it of the need in the near future also to face the challenges of internal pluralism.[19]

Translated by John Bowden

Notes

1. Cf. J. Bajzek, 'Nekaj znailnosti danasnje mladine', in *2000*, Ljubljana 1987, nos.35–36, 24–35; S. Hribar, 'Vrednote Mladih', in *Vrednote, Mevskofijski odbor za studente*, Ljubljana 1986, 88–122.
2. Cf. S. Gerjolj, *Ideologie und Bildung*, Justus-Liebig-Universität Giessen 1997.

3. Cf. A. Stres, 'Moralische Erneuerung erforderlich', in Norbert Sommer (ed.), *Der Traum aber bleibt*, Berlin 1992, 329–34.

4. Id., 'Kirche im demokratischen Staat am Beispiel Sloweniens', in Renovabis, *Säkulariserung und Pluralismus in Europa. Was wird aus der Kirche*, Freising 1998, 138–51.

5. This situation can be compared with that after the collapse of Nazism, when just as many people had to concede that they had done too little against Hitler's totalitarianism (cf. D. Baake, *Die 13–18 Jährigen*, Weinheim and Basel 1983).

6. Young people need resistance. They also know that this can hurt them. But they also know that only in this way can they acquire the necessary experience to discover a realizable harmony with themselves, their fellow men and women and the world (cf. P. Schellenbaum, *Gottesbilder – Religion, Psychoanalyse, Tiefenpsychologie*, Munich ³1993).

7. Cf. F. Rode, *Spomin, Zavest, Nart Cerkve na Slovenskem*, Ljubljana 1995.

8. Cf. V. Pronik, *Veroueènci in spoved*, Ljubljana 2000.

9. Source: Aufbruch (New Departures) 1998 (Vinko Potocnik).

10. Accordingly 'the legislator made the basic principle that all changes in education and training should take place in stages' (*Ministrstvo za solstvo in sport. Bela knjiga o vzgoji in izobrazevanju v Republiki Sloveniji*, Ljublana 1995, 13).

11. Cf. *Zakon o organizaciji in financiranju vzgoje in izobrazevanja s komentarjem*, Ljubljana 1997, no.86.

12. Cf. ibid., no.87.

13. Cf. ibid., no.72; also P.Zgaga, 'Pouevanje in Avtonomija', in *Kaj Honemo in Kaj Zoremo*, Ljubljana 1992, 25.

14. Cf . *Ministrstvo za solstvo in sport* (n.10), 27.

15. In the first year (1998/99) this subject was not taught in any of the eighteen experimental schools, as too few pupils were interested in it (cf. S. Rogelj-Petriè, 'Sivlestra, Verouk in Verstva in Etika – Zmeda I Nenaklonjenost', *Delot*, 27 December 1999, 9).

16. This includes not only various ideological conceptions but also constructive and positive variants of solutions to problems which arouse a constructive sense of responsibility among children and young people, cf. J. J. Mitchell, *Adolescent Struggle for Selfhood and Identity*, Alberta, Calgary 1992.

17. 'If testimony to experience is one of the important pedagogical categories, then this is particularly true of experiences within religious education (G. Biemer, 'Auf dem Weg zu einer wirklichkeitshältigen Religionsdidaktik', in A. Biesinger and T. Schreijäck (eds), *Religionsunterricht heute*, Freiburg im Breisgau 1989, 264–7.

18. This question needs a thorough theological discussion. But in conversations about praxis the reason cited keeps appearing that by postponing confirmation to a high age one can keep the pupils in the educational process for longer.

19. Cf. Stres, 'Kirche im demokratischen Staat' (n.4), 140f.

Priests and Religious Orders

VINKO POTOCNIK

Attempts to marginalize or eliminate the church or religion have usually begun with attacks on the clergy. On the other hand, history teaches that renewals of religious and church life also usually begin with a renewal of the priesthood.

In the Eastern part of Europe, too, the hostility of the Communist regime to the church was first directed against bishops, priests and those in religious orders. Therefore we can rightly expect that the collapse of the Communist system which took place ten years ago also found specific expression in the question of priests. The priests experienced the sudden end of (official) pressure in a particularly marked way. Earlier restrictions on religious activity, though they had already been diminishing for some time, were replaced by new possibilities of religious life and the priestly mission.

However, we have to ask whether such a sudden and at the same time far-reaching change in the social and religious situation does not represent a real 'culture shock' for the priest. After decades in which his priestly role was above all subordinate to the fight of the religious community for survival and their own survival, was this not a crisis of priestly identity? What do believers and people generally expect of the priest and of the church in such a time? What can be said about the question of priests from a demographic perspective? These remarks on the questions and dilemmas posed for the mission of priests and religious orders in the post-socialist countries of Eastern Europe are based on some religious and demographic data[1] and also on the international investigation on religion in Central and Eastern Europe made by the organization Aufbruch (New Departures).[2] This survey is limited to the situation of Catholic priests.

I. Some data

Today around 340 million inhabitants – half the population of Europe – live in the overall area of the twenty countries of Central and Eastern Europe.

These do not represent a uniform cultural sphere but are very different geo-
graphically, historically, economically, ethnically, culturally and in religious
terms.[3] Approximately 72 million, i.e. around 22% of the population, are
(baptized) Catholics. But about half of the Catholics in this part of Europe
(36 million) live in one country – Poland. Outside Poland, Catholics are still
in the majority in Lithuania (86%), Slovenia (92%) and Hungary (63%); in
other European countries they are in the minority (for the most part alongside the Orthodox churches, elsewhere alongside Protestantism and here
and there alongside Islam). In Russia and Estonia they do not represent even
1% of the population. They form a rather larger proportion of the population (17%) in Bosnia and Herzegovina and also in Albania.

In this sphere of the former Communist totalitarian regime with its
plurality of churches and religions, religious life is organized within the
framework of 161 Catholic dioceses and 25,930 parishes. An average diocese
has around 2 million inhabitants;[4] approximately 450,000 Catholics live in
on average 170 parishes. An average parish numbers 2,700 Catholics.

In 1996, 41,800 diocesan priests and priests in religious orders were active
in this area. That represents on average 266 priests per diocese, which is not
very different from the European average (299 priests per diocese). However, because of the gigantic difference in the number of priests between
individual dioceses, this figure does not mean much. Thus an average
diocese in Poland has more than 600 diocesan priests and priests in religious
orders, whereas dioceses in the Russian Federation, in White Russia,
Estonia, Moldavia, Bulgaria, Yugoslavia, Albania or Macedonia do not even
have 100 priests per diocese. That merely indicates the varied backgrounds
against which Catholic priests live and work.

The question whether there is a greater or lesser shortage of priests in this
part of Europe can be answered by citing the number of inhabitants (8,130)
or Catholics (1,720) per priest. By comparison with the European average –
one priest to 3,186 inhabitants or 1,317 Catholics – the figures indicate a
much lower presence of diocesan priests or priests in religious orders in
Eastern Europe.

This statement about a shortage of priests is also justified by information
about parishes without a resident pastor: there are more than 2,000 of these
in the former Communist countries, i.e. 20% of all parishes. The relatively
largest number of vacant parishes is in the Czech Republic (as high as 62%),
in the Russian Federation (48%), in Hungary (36%) and in Lithuania
(31%).

A general observation may be made about the number of priestly vocations. After the beginning of the Communist era their number diminished very considerably everywhere, partly because of the great pressure on the church (sometimes they halved in some decades). After a certain time – in some places still in the time of Communism,[5] and elsewhere only after the change – as a rule there was a jump in the rise of priestly vocations, though things soon settled down. We can see this phenomenon as an attempt to catch up with what had been neglected; above all it is a sign of the end of Communism. In a third of the former Communist countries the number of priestly vocations is still rising, but in most other countries the pendulum has swung the other way. In Croatia and even more in Poland, the most Catholic of all the countries in transition, the number of vocations to the clergy has been declining slowly but steadily over this decade.

II. Priests and members of religious orders

1. The relation between diocesan priests and priests in religious orders

Priests in religious orders differ in their specific mission and also in their life-style. Any observer can easily note that the life of the diocesan priest is more orientated on the individual and that of the priest in religious orders more on the community. In a sense the mission of the priests in religious orders seeks to be more radically true to the gospel and 'within the church', whereas pastoral priests – as well as preaching, celebrating the liturgy and administering the sacraments – also devote themselves to various kinds of pastoral work and organization, including relations with the 'outside' world. Therefore the latter are more prepared than priests in religious orders for compromises with the world.

The quantitative relationship between the two groups may itself be relevant to understanding the church, since – at least to a certain degree – it indicates the strength of one or other way of 'being the church'. In the countries of Central and Eastern Europe there are 32,953 diocesan priests and 9,848 priests in religious orders. That is a ratio of 100:31; this ratio is notably less than the European average of 100:43.[6]

Among the twenty former socialist countries there are six in which priests in religious orders are in the majority. However, if we look more closely we see that these are countries with a relatively small number of Catholics and priests: Bulgaria, Albania, Bosnia and Herzegovina, the Russian Federation, Moldavia and White Russia, where Catholicism has a marked diaspora status.

Because of the lack of information from the Communist period it is impossible to establish whether this relationship has perhaps changed in favour of one group or the other. At any rate the proportion of priests in religious orders in this part of Europe need not necessarily have diminished. At least in some countries[7] it is possible to note a relative rise in the number of priests in religious orders for the Communist period.

However, the proportion of priests in religious orders remains notably below the European average in the former socialist countries. An explanation of this can be sought in several directions. In many places Communism banned the religious orders. An underground existence remained possible only with great sacrifice. In particular, it was impossible to foster vocations. In some of these countries the religious orders had been heavily affected by the reforms of the emperor and king Joseph II (1780–1790), who dissolved most religious houses. Possibly the proximity of the Eastern Church, in which the life of the religious orders has a special significance, also played a role; thus the Catholic orders could not become more prominent because they did not emphasize their Catholic identity. Protestantism, with its negative attitude to the religious life, certainly also had an influence. Finally, we must remember that the pressure on the church to some degree reduced the need for the special character of religious orders; most priests were isolated anyway and therefore to some degree were forced into 'the religious life'.

By contrast, possibly many priests in religious orders orientated themselves on parish activity because of the special circumstances and needs. But this assumption is not confirmed by data; these show that in the sphere of the post-socialist countries priests in religious orders looked after 2,113 parishes, 8% of all parishes. The proportion of priests in religious orders in charge of parishes is very much at the European level – except in the countries of the Catholic diaspora, which have a far higher level.[8]

At all events, not least because of the political pressure, the life and activity of the two groups seems to have come together or been quite unified, especially as in the struggle for survival there was a concentration on the necessities. Therefore in the time of Communism the specific characteristics and charisms of the priests in religious orders or diocesan priests were expressed far less.

2. Men and women in religious orders, deacons and catechists

In the countries of the former European Communist block today, alongside priests in religious orders there are 2,700 men in orders who are not priests. Thus there are 12,565 men in religious orders, priests and non-priests; 22% of these live out their charism in the order without priestly consecration.

In the same area 41,584 women also live and work in religious orders, a number corresponding to that of the priests in religious orders and diocesan priests put together. There are fewer priests than women in religious orders in Hungary and the Ukraine, around a third more in Croatia, the Czech Republic and Slovakia.

In Eastern Europe there are currently 21,000 catechists, men and women, which doubtless indicates that the church has opened up to new pastoral callings. That is also confirmed by the presence of around 230 permanent deacons in these countries. The data cited show that priesthood and the life of the religious orders in these countries has not only survived the Communist era but also kept its basic structures intact. At present its vitality is shown not only in the demographic quantitative sense but also at the level of adaptation to the new conditions.

III. Expectations attached to the church and priests

To some degree it is up to the priests what ideas, expectations and wishes people have about and for them. Here the change has brought a new challenge. The more or less stereotyped images of the mission of the priest on the one hand and the actual or 'new' role of a priest in the post-socialist period on the other can easily come into conflict. Therefore it is interesting to ask what the inhabitants of Eastern Europe expect of the church or of priests. What roles do they allow the church and priests?

Empirical data from the 'New Departures' investigation[9] indicate that despite lengthy attempts to discredit the priests or the church, most inhabitants of the post-Communist countries assign them important roles. Most (around a half) believe that the church can offer answers to many individual and intimate questions, e.g. to questions of morality or the meaning of life; on social questions around a quarter to a third of people believe the church competent to offer answers.

However, the readiness to recognize that the church can exercise these rules does not always mean that the church or the priests should do so. Almost half the population of the post-Communist countries expects a pastoral word on questions of personal morality and concrete social questions, but a far smaller proportion expects statements on public issues and politics. Here we can note a paradoxical opposition: among religious people the number of those who emphasize the various competences of the church is larger than the number of those who expect these competences also to be realized. However, the non-religious believe less in the capacities of the church and the priests, but expect a greater contribution from them towards solving various questions.

Has the church said too much, too little or just enough in the time after the change to democracy? The following picture emerges. Rather more than half those surveyed think that over the last ten years (since the church has been able to express itself) what the church has said has been right; the other half is polarized into groups which say either 'too much' or 'too little'. Here, in the Ukraine and the former DDR, those who want the church to say more in public dominate; and in Romania, the Czech Republic and Hungary the two opinions are equally represented. In the other countries (Poland, Slovenia, Croatia, Lithuania and Slovakia) those who think that the church has said too much at this time predominate. Thus in these societies there is often clear opposition to the public involvement of the church. All this information indicates a very complex reality which is mixed up with detachment from the church and priests and a great indifference to them. A good quarter of the adult population is not interested in what happens to or in the church.

However, the data indicate people who treasure the church and its priests and expect much of them, though their attitude is becoming increasingly critical. In this case the information about dissatisfaction with the Catholic Church does not mean a fundamentally negative attitude to the church or even repudiation of the church, but above all the desire for it to change.

IV. On expectations

For the church and also for the priests in the countries of Eastern Europe, the collapse of Communism is a special sign of the time. With it ended an era which initially led to a marked decrease in the number of priests. The regimes made efforts to demote the social status of the priests as far as possible and at the same time to weaken the religious communities. But the regimes did not succeed in giving themselves a significance, which was certainly one of the causes of the gradual inner decay of the social structure.

A special sign of the time for the priest's mission is also given by people with their ideas about the priesthood and with the expectations they have for the church. Here there can be tensions, as the priest's mission cannot simply be adapted to the expectations of people or to the 'demands of the market'.[10]

Therefore a special task of the priest in the post-Communist era is neither to withdraw into the pre-Communist period nor simply to adopt the pattern of Western Christianity, but to pay attention to the expectations and needs of people locally. Here the priest should not attempt to take on the role of a psychologist, psychotherapist, social worker or other member of the helping professions in place of his priestly task. The priest is no longer the only educated person. There is a series of new professions in competition with which he would certainly lose, since they devote themselves exclusively to people in need. Above all the priest would lose the roots of his identity as a priest or a religious.

The transition to a democratic society offers priests the possibility of different specializations, especially the development of different charisms. That will certainly result in a growing differentiation within the ranks of priests. The burdens of a life which is set apart and perhaps isolated may well grow as a result. Therefore the development of communal forms of life for priests and members of religious orders will become an increasingly important task.

One of the most demanding tasks of Catholic priests will certainly be the education of Catholic lay people to assume their mission at the heart of society. People's expectations in this direction are very low. Therefore the priest cannot just adapt his mission to expectations but must stand above them or listen to 'higher' expectations. Here the experiences from the Communist period are certainly valuable, since in the end here too there is a struggle for justice and freedom.

Translated by John Bowden

Notes

1. *Annuarium Statisticum Ecclesiae 1996*, Libreria Editrice Vaticana 1998. Other statistical data on the church come from various issues of the same source.
2. Cf. M. Tomka and P. Zulehner, *Religion in den Reformländern Ost (Mittel) Europa*, Ostfildern 1999.
3. This is the area from the Urals and the Black Sea in the East to the Alps (Slovenia) in the West, from the Baltic in the north to the southern Balkans (Albania, Macedonia and Bulgaria) in the south.
4. The reason for this high average is the size of the dioceses in the Russian Federation. In Poland, where there are forty-three dioceses, an individual

diocese has around 900,000 inhabitants. In terms of population, on average the smallest dioceses are in Croatia.

5. In Slovenia there was an explosive growth in priestly vocations at the end of the 1960s and the beginning of the 1970s which coincided with the post-conciliar period in the church and with a certain liberalization of the regime.

6. The proportion of priests in religious orders to diocesan priests is lower in Europe than in any other continent. But this proportion has been stable for some time, whereas it has been falling everywhere else in the world. Globally, 35% of all priests are in religious orders.

7. Thus for example a gradual rise in the proportion of priests in religious orders over the whole Communist period has been noted for Slovenia and for Hungary. Cf. M. Tomka and E. Révay, 'Priests and Religious Orders', in *Social Report 1998*, Budapest 1999, 227–47.

8. Only in rare cases are parishes led by men in religious orders who are not priests (6), by women in orders (3), or by laity (8).

9. Cf. Tomka and Zulehner, *Religion in den Reformländern* (n.2), 105–30. This sociological investigation covers half the countries of Central and Eastern Europe in transition.

10. Cf. Jakov Juki, *Budnost religije*, Split 1991, 32–3.

Religion and Media

LÁSZLÓ LUKÁCS

The political changes in Europe meant a double challenge for the post-Communist countries. They had to catch up with the Western economic market and at the same time overtake the speeding rhythm of modernization in the first world. One of the most important characteristics of the time is the dawn of the new information era.[1] The developed countries entered the multimedia revolution, and the post-Communist countries had to follow them without any real preparation. Religion and more concretely the churches in the region had to face this new phenomenon.

I. The heritage of the past

Though Communist ideology and the party system was basically the same all over Eastern Europe, there were great differences in the situations of the churches in different countries. One extreme is the example of Poland, where the church has always been very strong, with fervent Christian faith and a marked influence on society (second only to Ireland in Europe). The other extreme is Albania, the country where religion was officially and legally forbidden. Or, as far as the churches themselves are concerned, the Greek Uniate Church was suppressed in most countries of Eastern Europe by law, while other churches could continue their activity, even if in a limited manner.

The religious (and more specifically the Catholic) media landscape also varied from country to country. If we try to make a comparison, we could say that apart from the excellent and well-established Catholic media of Poland, the relatively free church press in Yugoslavia, the restricted but existing press in East Germany and Hungary, there was nothing like Catholic (or religious) media in other Communist countries, so they had to start their activities from a zero-point in 1989-90.

1. Microcommunication – underground

Despite all the differences, some general characteristics can be observed. In the times of oppression in these countries hardly any free communication was possible on the institutional and official levels, either in society as a whole or in the churches. In most of these countries the institutional churches were put under strict control and could exist only within a limited framework. The free cells under totalitarian dictatorships were the small underground base communities, among them those of believers. These small groups were the centres of communion and communication, for a small number of people but in a very personal and intensive manner. A dynamic micro-communication system functioned with little or no macro-communication among the different base communities and with public society. The result was that in many of the churches in the region there was hardly any experience of social communication. The most precise data bank was kept by the secret police and in the archives of the state secretariats for the churches.

2. Everyday communication within the church

The political changes granted freedom of religion and made the re-organization of the traditional churches possible. At the same time new religious groups appeared, partly small evangelical churches, partly religious groups claiming to be the followers of some religion from the Far East but in a particular European fashion. These groups imported an effective marketing strategy, often more advanced than the traditional and sometimes old-fashioned methods of the Christian denominations.

The traditional churches had to face and overcome a great many difficulties. At first sight the lack of financial resources, of the necessary infrastructure and of trained media experts called for the most urgent solution. However, the first-aid actions proved that the needs and problems are rooted more deeply. The first problem may be called 'persecution syndrome', which has haunted the churches for years even after the changes. It was difficult to forget the times of oppression and persecution and change the attitudes caused by the pressure of discrimination. Consequently the oppressors were blamed for all the failures and mistakes in the churches. A system of self-control; an examination of conscience for the past; strategic planning; a realistic analysis of the situation; a feasibility study for the future – all these were replaced by the heroism and faithfulness of the victims. The time of oppression was a favourable time for charismatic personalities and private adventures, but destroyed the need for co-operation, organized structures, flexible adjustment to the external situation. The outstanding partisans of the past often could not be enrolled into a regular army. As a result many people in the churches thought they had a right to unlimited subsidy, without a realistic budget and regular control.

The second greatest difficulty was the lack of media awareness. A new mentality had to develop about information and communication, not only in the mass media, but first and foremost in everyday religious activity. The churches of the reform countries had to change their underground mentality and adjust themselves to public life. In the past, secrecy and hiddenness had been the condition for survival. Entering the atmosphere of freedom, both church officials and believers had to learn that the fundamental requirement for communication is the exchange of information. 'The normal flow of life and the smooth functioning of government within the Church require a steady two-way flow of information between the ecclesiastical authorities at all levels and the faithful as individuals and as organized groups.'[2] Western churches offered financial subsidy but also their know-how for management and communication. More than once, however, the former was expected and accepted, but the latter was refused or viewed with mistrust and reluctance. Both partners had to learn each other's language and understand the differing views and realities.

Churches in Eastern Europe needed the (re)creation of inner-church public opinion: a 'glass-house' atmosphere where all activities are visible and accountable and where all the members of the churches are invited to active participation. The circulation of information started slowly within the churches. A long learning process was needed to acquire the contemporary techniques of management, conference culture, decision-making processes and publicity in order to achieve better co-operation within their own organizations and communities.

The first task at the beginning of the 1990s was thus to help these churches to introduce adequate forms of modern administration and management; to ensure the smooth flow of information within different institutions and communities, among parishes and dioceses; to supply diocesan centres with all the data needed to make proper decisions with the help of a functioning system of reporting, of collecting and preserving data of church life, etc. It took a long time and much effort to raise a new awareness of communication, to build up the fundamental infrastructure and acquire the administrative skill necessary for such basic communication.

II. The recovery of social communication

The aim of all churches was to reconstruct the full range of religious press activity (both printed and electronic) activity. However, there was no strategic plan for the pastoral work of the media, so the religious media could not develop in a systematic and well-designed way, following the guidelines of an overall project.[3] The growth of the media happened in a more organic way, like trees and bushes in a forest: heroic efforts, but also some inconsistent and unsuccessful attempts; flourishing branches, but also barren plants are found in this landscape.[4]

Roughly speaking, the last decade can be divided into two periods. The first five to six years are characterized by the initial attempts and the establishment of the different religious media productions.[5] The religious media started to function normally in the second half of the decade, and the wounds of the past are still to be felt in several respects. In the past three or four years their achievement can be taken to be adequate by the standards of the media generally in the respective countries.

1. News agencies

News agencies offer the basic source for all media. Still, their unique importance for the religious press was discovered only slowly, and even today the quality of their production is not high enough. Several efforts have been made to create a network of information offices in different countries – with no real success.[6] Their work is often jeopardized by the lack of media awareness. Local (diocesan, etc.) media offices do not function effectively and cannot provide sufficient material in their reports. With very few exceptions, the secular media do not use their reports as primary sources but try to find more direct ways of getting information about religious affairs.

2. The print media

The church press (and this is true for the publication of books, too) was completely suppressed or strictly limited and controlled in most countries of Eastern Europe. Because of the Marxist hegemony in culture, hardly any Christians had the chance to study the arts in general or communication in particular. (As a result the percentage of Christians is much less among those who studied literature or fine arts or philosophy than among those who studied engineering or medicine.) The printed and electronic media were in the hands of the party state. Consequently at the beginning there were very few if any Christian experts who could restart anything like a religious press (and most of them did not have sufficient knowledge of theology, because there was no opportunity of studying theology or even of finding any books on theology).

When the political changes made free publication possible, doctors of medicine, engineers, teachers, students or other intellectuals with much good will and enthusiasm, with fervent Christian commitment but with no professional knowledge, started to edit religious monthlies and weeklies. While the Catholic media field in Western Europe had an immense wealth of professional know-how, an elaborate network for publications and an adequate financial background, in the East a few lone pioneers led a desperate struggle for economic survival, for improving their professional quality, for the training of young journalists. Now there are more and more experts working for the religious press – with an adequate training in journalism. Still, the training of journalists is a top priority even today.

The number of religious publications (weeklies, monthlies, quarterlies) grew rapidly during the decade, but their circulation was diminishing in most post-Communist countries. By now there are several national and a great many diocesan weeklies and monthlies in all post-Communist countries, even in countries like Belarus, Bulgaria and Albania. The European part of Russia has had a weekly since 1994 and since 1995 there has been another weekly for the Catholics in Siberia (200,000 in number, but in area the biggest diocese in the world).

Behind the promising results, the surprising but also embarrassing riches of publications, there are some tensions and difficulties, too. In several countries there is hardly any co-ordination among the publications, no dialogue among the publishing houses and editorial offices, no survey of the real needs of readers, no analysis of the financial possibilities. The question becomes unavoidable: who has the authority and responsibility to decide which publications should be subsidized and which should be stopped? Which areas of pastoral life are neglected or forgotten? Is the content and language of the religious press really adjusted to the changing desires and reading habits of believers? How can the religious press find a language capable of being understood by ordinary people? How can the religious press break out of the ghetto of pious slogans? Sooner or later the religious press has to face all the challenges familiar to Western media, first of all the cruel laws of the free-market system. A new and reasonable project for the written press and a pastoral plan for the media seems to be unavoidable.

3. Book publishing

Under the Communist regime only Samisdat publications and some theological books smuggled from abroad were accessible to a very small circle of
readers in most countries. In several places not even the most important
documents (e.g. missals or other liturgical books, the documents of Vatican
II) were translated into the vernacular. The scene changed in the first half of
the 1990s, but there is still an immense shortage of theological and religious
books: a gap of four to six decades has to be filled.

At the same time the book market is much larger than before. A large
number of works – both classical and modern – have been translated, on
philosophical and religious but also on pseudo-religious subjects. Alongside
serious books of theology and philosophy one can find all types of esoteric
books as well. People can now experience at first hand what freedom of
expression means. Any views can be expressed and propagated: those with a
true religious content, but also those with false and anti-religious ideas. Any
type of sensation is welcome and the churches are favourite targets of
sensation-mongers. Religion today finds itself in an environment completely
different from that of the past. Under the Marxist hegemony the media
were controlled and directed by the Party. Any attack on religion or on a
particular church was carefully prepared and planned, as part of the political
strategy. In our day all media are completely free: they can defend or attack
religion or any church; use or misuse religious feelings depending on their
own aims. Religion is no longer part of government policy. In the past
churches had to defend themselves against only one source of anti-religious
propaganda. Nowadays they are at the mercy of profit-making media
companies and exposed to every possible attack.

4. The electronic media

Religious programmes had virtually no access to television and radio in
Communist countries. After the change, the churches claimed air time in
both media, with more or less success. The time for religious programmes
differs from country to country, but in most places there is some regular
broadcasting time on national television and in the national radio programmes. (In most countries the production of these programmes is paid for
by the national radio or television company itself.) In the second half of the
decade – alongside the appearance of commercial channels – the churches
created private Christian radio stations. Most of them are to be found in
Poland, but Croatia, Slovenia and Slovakia also run private Catholic radio

stations. They are naturally in fierce competition with other stations and programmes.

Religious programmes produced by the national broadcasting companies are guaranteed by law, but these companies have lost their hegemony and are slowly being defeated by commercial channels. Serious religious programmes which can be set alongside real scientific, artistic and educational programmes are the last bastions of high culture: they are under continuous pressure from low-quality commercial productions which can often attract viewers more successfully.

The electronic media scene is similar to that of book and periodical publishing. Besides traditional Christian churches, different evangelical groups and every possible view with fake-religious allusions find their way on to the air, getting (or frequently buying) air time in different commercial channels. They mostly come from North America. That is why they have the financial sources and technical skills to produce attractive programmes. TV viewers really need the spirit of discernment to make a difference between true and false messengers of Christianity, between true religion and pseudo-religious programmes without any relationship to God. A lot of TV viewers, however, do not know religion at all and are easily confused about the essence of religion.

The challenge is immense. The sheer fact of possessing a certain amount of air-time is not sufficient if the programmes are not attractive enough to hold the attention of both believers and non-believers.

5. *The Internet*

The Internet was born in the past few years and it was adopted in Eastern Europe almost as fast as in the West. Almost all churches and several other religious groups have their own home pages. Some of them are bilingual (e.g. the Russian, the Croatian, the Hungarian pages), trying to break through the language barrier. Some are run by official church authorities, others by enthusiastic lay people or some religious order. The quality of their format and content is somewhat uneven, but they mostly respond to the challenges of the time and provide adequate, up-to-date and interesting material to Internet-surfers.

III. Future perspectives

The media in post-Communist countries have been modernized in the Western sense with all the consequences, good and bad; big multimedia enterprises are present throughout the region. The religious media have overcome the first difficulties. For their future success they have to heal all the wounds of the past and create a genuine atmosphere of communication.[7]

1. Wounds to be healed: fear and mistrust

After decades of persecution fear is still present as one of the typical syndromes of the adult population, especially of religious people. Three types of it are still present.

First, there is the suspicion or even fear of Western Europe, the churches included. Those who suffered for their faith under a totalitarian dictatorship regard the believers of the West as liberal, secularized persons, who betrayed true Christianity. This feeling has diminished but not yet disappeared, especially in the older generation.

Secondly, many church officials have a fear of journalists. Remembering some bitter experiences, they condemn all the journalists and all the media, blaming them for mishandling religion. The relationship between the church and the press is not unclouded in many countries. More patience and dialogue should be invested in creating better public relations for the churches.

Thirdly, most of the clergy have never been confronted with different views, and have little experience and skill in starting a dialogue with people with divergent viewpoints. In a monolithic society like the Communist regime, no culture of dialogue could develop. In the spirit of the Vatican II, Christians ought to learn to engage in dialogue with other religions and with all people of good-will.

2. The need for pastoral planning and co-operation in the media

A pastoral plan for social communications is urgently needed in all the churches. It should be based on a survey of the present situation of the country or region. It should then formulate the fundamental goals and principles of the religious media. What is the role of the media in the life of the church, in the dialogue with the world? As a further step an adequate strategy should be elaborated for all types of media, taking into account needs and possibilities, challenges and dangers, but also finances, personnel, formation, etc.

Following *Communio et progressio*, the most important aim of communication is to foster dialogue within the church, to create a public opinion within the church and to strengthen the church as communion. The second task is no less important: a dialogue among religions, among the churches and in society. Eastern Europe has also become part of the information society: can the churches find and keep their own voice in the growing choir of multimedia? This is the greatest challenge for them in the future, and the past can hardly be blamed any longer for possible failure.

Notes

1. Martin Bangemann, *Europe and the Global Information Society*, Luxembourg 1994; *Europe's Way to the Information Society, Updated Version to 24 January 1996*, ISPO; Karl Steinbuch, *Die informierte Gesellschaft*, 1966; id., *Informationsflut — Probleme der gegenwärtigen Massenkommunikation*, 1979.

2. *Communio et Progressio* 120.

3. *Aetatis Novae* urged bishops' conferences to create their own pastoral plan for the media and even gave general guidelines for its elaboration – realization on the national and diocesan level is still awaited in most countries. Cf. also Victor Sunderaj (ed.), *Pastoral Planning for Social Communication*, Montreal 1998.

4. László Lukács, 'Probleme nach dem Umbruch', in *Kirchenpresse am Ende des Jahrtausends, Berichte aus 15 Ländern Europas und aus den Vereinigten Staaten*, Paderborn 1992, 117–20.

5. László Lukács, 'Social Communications in Central and Eastern Europe', *Mediaforum* 2/1997; id., *Die Medien in der katholischen Kirche Osteuropas von 1990 bis 2000*, Communicatio Socialis Heft 4.

6. In the mid-1990s, Kathpress of Austria tried to create a network of news 'agencies' with the neighbouring Central-European countries. The strongest news agency exists in Poland, but there are news agencies in Croatia (IKA), in Hungary (Magyar Kurir), in Ukraine (ARI), in Russia (BLI) and Bosnia (KTA).

7. Philippe Breton, *L'utopie de la communication*, Paris 1997.

Still Building Bridges: Eastern Europe's Church in the World Church

A decade after the collapse of Communist rule, conditions for religious life contrast sharply in Eastern and Central Europe, as attempts continue to define its rightful place in the region's new democracies. The church has consolidated its position in Lithuania, Poland, Slovakia and Croatia, but become marginalized in the Czech Republic and Hungary, while in much of the former Soviet Union it has had to rebuild from scratch, starved of resources in an unsupportive environment. Yet the practical record is even more mixed. Although Hungary's Catholic Church clashed with the Socialist-led government over property restitutions and budget allocations, its parliament became the first to approve a full-scale treaty with the Vatican in December 1997. In the Pope's native Poland, by contrast, a 1993 Concordat took five years to be ratified by parliament.

I. Wide variations

Wide variations are evident, from press to education. Whereas Poland is home to a flourishing network of Catholic newspapers and radios, the chairman of Slovenia's Bishops Conference, Archbishop Franc Rode, has warned that the media are still controlled by the 'old authorities' and hostile to the church.[1] While Hungary's 180 Catholic schools are to obtain the same subsidies as state schools, neighbouring Slovakia's are expected to be church-funded. In Poland, state wages are paid to 20,000 priests who teach the catechism in schools. In the Czech Republic, the state has paid salaries to all registered clergy since the eighteenth century.

Differences are also striking when it comes to moral issues. Polish law cut officially registered abortions to 310 nation-wide in 1998, whereas around 70,000 are performed annually in Hungary and 1.2 million in neighbouring Romania.

Despite the contrasts, a sense of region-wide identity nevertheless persists. It has been largely shaped by Communist-era experiences, but it also reflects shared emotions as to where East European Catholics stand in relation to the wider universal church.

The Catholic Church experienced Communist rule differently depending on its strengths and weaknesses in each country. In Poland, it was targeted because of its identification with patriotic values, whereas in the Czech lands and Hungary it was attacked because of its perceived link with a reactionary anti-national order. In Lithuania, Slovakia and Croatia it was identified as a bastion of nationalism; in Ukraine, Romania and Belarus it was associated with troublesome minorities.

The church's survival was vitally helped by its link to Rome. But it can be argued that no Pope ever quite found the right response. Pius XI and Pius XII both tried to counter Communism by confronting it – the first branding it 'intrinsically evil', the second excommunicating its collaborators with a 1949 Holy Office decree. Yet this polarized attitudes and drove Catholics into opposition, making it easier for Communist regimes to depict church members as conspirators and traitors.

John XXIII applied the 'medicine of mercy rather than severity', and urged Catholics to distinguish 'false philosophical theories' from the 'practical measures' to which they gave rise.[2] Yet some believed that his calls for peaceful coexistence helped to legitimize Soviet rule.

Paul VI tried to 'save what could be saved' by showing Communists what they could gain from concessions in an era of *Détente*. But the policy of bartering 'small step' concessions was contested by those who believed that it eroded the church's moral authority while producing few pastoral benefits.

The Second Vatican Council which Pope Paul closed was seen in a distinctive way in Eastern Europe. Having had trouble gaining passports to attend, most bishops felt discriminated against by language barriers and looked down on by Western counterparts. They were also sceptical about the Council's documents, seeing their diagnosis of contemporary church issues as overwhelmingly Western-dominated.

Several East European bishops endorsed the Council's decision not to condemn Communism, believing this would be counter-productive. But many were suspicious that Vatican II failed even to mention it by name. Talk of a 'new attitude' was widely derided. So were phrases in the Church's Pastoral Constitution, *Gaudium et spes*, such as 'nations which favour a' collective economy'. The very issue of religious freedom had a starkness in

Eastern Europe which seemed barely accounted for in the genteel contents of *Dignitatis humanae*, which made no more than a passing reference to 'forms of government' which 'strive to deter the citizens from professing their religion'.[3]. Far more attention was devoted in Council documents to North-South issues. It was one symptom of what many saw as the Western Church's failure to understand their plight.

This was not entirely just. Important practical and psychological support was provided throughout the Communist period to underground church groups in Poland and other countries. Meanwhile, charges of neglect were much harsher against the Protestant-dominated World Council of Churches, whose silence over human rights abuses is still remembered with bitterness today.

Yet the impression remained widespread that Rome and Western church leaders failed to give sufficient support. An internal report prepared for Poland's Bishops' Conference in 1974 voiced bitterness at the 'conformist attitude to Marxism' evident in Vatican and Western church documents. The 'conspiracy of silence' about crimes committed against the human conscience, it argued, would only make Communism more aggressive.[4] The report was written under the auspices of Cardinal Karol Wojtyla of Krakow. When he was elected Pope in 1978, the situation began to change.

John Paul II had a far better knowledge than his predecessors of Communist methods, and a keener grasp of what might be done to counter the psychological complexes which the regimes exploited. He knew the Communist rulers grew stronger when challenged by force but had no answer to peaceful moral resistance. By the time of his first Polish homecoming in 1979, it was clear that a breach had been made in the East-West wall cemented at the 1945 Yalta Conference, with its naive prediction of a 'continuing and growing understanding between East and West'.[5] It was to be widened by successive Polish visits in 1983 and 1987, which revealed the Pope's capacity to mobilize the church as a social force independently of the wielders of power.

Nineteenth- century pontiffs, mesmerized by images of destruction from the French Revolution to Paris Commune, had feared the potential of spontaneous social movements. But the Pope saw them as allies – a creative energy which the church could harness and direct for godly purposes. The 'movements of solidarity' of which he spoke in his 1981 encyclical *Laborem exercens* were not foes, but friends of Christianity.[6] They could be used to divest Communist ideals of their totalitarian and ideological distortions, and to transform the system's illusory values into real ones.

It was his effectiveness in the struggle with Communism which explains why a pope sometimes viewed in the West as a reactionary figure with a revisionist view of Vatican II was seen in the East as a champion of human freedom who had given the Council's concern for humanity a dynamic, unexpected application.

When democracy returned to Eastern Europe, it was natural to hope that elements of the region's courageous Christianity would survive in the new post-Communist era. 'Today, we stand before the ruins of one of the many towers of Babel in human history,' John Paul II told Czech Catholics in April 1990. 'The Church's solidarity with the persecuted has strengthened its moral authority, and you hold in your hands the capital of merits amassed by those who sacrificed their life and freedom. This is truly a rich inheritance. Do not squander it!'[7]

The Pope was aware of the immense historic tasks the church in Eastern and Central Europe now faced. It had to breathe new life into Catholic parishes, renew religious orders, revive seminary vocations, provide education and catechesis, encourage the reintegration of lay movements, reawaken ecumenical bonds and reassert its presence in public life. He believed the task would be made easier by an 'exchange of gifts' between East and West, building on his own past efforts to reinstall a sense of Europe's wider unity.

Western Catholics could offer their know-how in areas from parish finances to media relations. East European Catholics could offer, in the words of the Czech Cardinal Miloslav Vlk, 'the experience of a God who is close and a living faith strengthened by Communist persecutions, as well as the heroism of people in a suffering Church and the empirically tested conviction that social development is impossible without a spiritual dimension'.[8]

Putting these fine-sounding formulations into practice, however, was to prove arduous and difficult. The Eastern experience of persecution, however moving, had little direct relevance to the daily lives of Western middle-class Christians. Meanwhile, there were key East European priorities, such as the reintegration of official and underground church structures, where Western expertise had little to offer.

II. Historic tasks

The euphoria of 1989–90 soon vanished anyway in bitter struggles over the shape of state and society which overshadowed the church's wider social role. The confidently predicted 'transition' looked more like a trek from an

uncertain present to an undefined future. In the early 1990s, Eastern
Europe's client relationship with the West seemed to be reflected among
Catholics as well.

Since then, two European Synods in 1991 and 1999 have attempted to
articulate common problems, ranging from evangelization and ecumenism
to migration and the challenge of Islam. Ecclesiastical reorganizations have
boosted the role of East Europeans in international Church fora. Post-
Communist countries now provide more than half of Europe's 36 Catholic
Bishops' Conferences, while the St Gallen-based Council of Catholic
Episcopates of Europe (CCEE) contains a strong East European presence.

The Vatican has diplomatic relations with 28 former Communist states in
Eastern Europe, including 16 ex-Soviet republics. The Pope has travelled
to 14 countries, including traditionally Orthodox Georgia and Romania,
paying 8 visits to his native Poland and 2 each to Hungary, Slovenia,
Slovakia and the Czech Republic.

It can be argued that both sides have gone some way towards responding
to mutual needs. Western church bodies, such as *Renovabis* and *Kirche in
Not* in Germany, have continued to provide generous material help to post-
Communist Christian communities. For its part, the church in Eastern and
Central Europe has helped to ease the burden of declining missions and
vocations. Priests are working at senior levels in western Russia and Siberia
from Slovakia's central Banska Bystrica diocese alone, where the average
clergy age of thirty-five is Europe's lowest. However, pride of place is
occupied by Poland, which sends 12% of its priests abroad. A growing proportion of the 3,000 Polish priests currently working in 92 countries are
based in post-Communist countries, including 146 in neighbouring Belarus
and 150 in Ukraine. In 1999, Poles made up 73 of the 115 priests under
Archbishop Tadeusz Kondrusiewicz in European Russia, where their
number had doubled in two years. They accounted for half the priests and
nuns in the church's Irkutsk-based eastern Siberia apostolic administration,
which is headed by a Polish Divine Word bishop, Jerzy Mazur, and a similar
proportion in Kazakhstan, which is home to two Polish bishops and a Polish
Vatican nuncio. In other ex-Soviet republics, Polish is the first language
after Russian in Catholic parishes and associations. Close links are
maintained with the Polish Church in catechesis and education, liturgy and
seminary training. However, the greatest number of Polish priests were
ministering in Western countries, ranging from 472 in Italy and 430 in
Germany to 18 in Spain and 17 in Sweden. With a third of Polish citizens
attending church regularly, the country's Catholic clergy increased by 14%

in the 1990s to over 30,000, and the church's 7,000 seminarians make up a quarter of Europe's total. In France, by contrast, where 148 Polish priests are working, only one in 10 Catholics attend mass and the church has around 1,000 seminarians. Having boasted 45,000 priests in 1945, France is expected to have 8–10,000 by 2005.[9]

Yet the mentality and outlook of the East European Church still have trouble finding acceptance in the West. Western Catholics find it difficult to understand why suffering and persecution are rooted in the East European identity, just as East Europeans have difficulty appreciating why apparent doctrinal abstractions matter in the West. The search for unity looks set to continue for the foreseeable future.

The Western Church remains wary of the pressure exerted by zealous, missionizing priests from Eastern Europe, whose criticisms of 'Western materialism' often reflect a weak grasp of the complex spiritual geography of Western societies. Some Western Catholics view them as a disruptive element, representing an antiquated model of church-state relations which contradicts democracy, and an authoritarian, politicized approach to religious affiliations which jars with the church's carefully nurtured place in the pluralistic West.

East European church leaders are also perceived to be obsessed with their own domestic affairs, seeing the world in simplistic colours and showing little interest in wider issues. The fact that most major European renewal movements originated in the West suggests that the post-modern Western hunger for spirituality is not the same as a craving for East European Catholicism.

Western church attitudes to Eastern and Central Europe are also affected by criticism of the Pope. Polish church perspectives have played their part in John Paul II's attempts to discipline church dissenters and bring liberation theology under control. Meanwhile, Polish church lobbies were widely believed to have been instrumental in the appointment of conservative church leaders in Austria and elsewhere, some of whom proved deeply controversial.

III. Different experiences

Yet East Europeans have their complaints too. The most common is that the Western Church has not understood Communism. In the pre-War Soviet Union alone, 200,000 Orthodox priests, monks and nuns were slaughtered and 45,000 churches destroyed in the greatest persecution of Christian history. But Western Catholics are accused of a Hegelian tendency to tailor their perception of reality to suit their preferred assumptions. Just as the Western Left by-passes Eastern Europe, since it reveals the failure of applied Marxism, so the vibrancy of East European faith must be ignored, since it exposes the weakness of Western Catholicism.

Some East Europeans complain that Western Catholics see them as an amorphous bloc, showing no interest in the specifics of each country. They are also fearful that liberal Western influences will superimpose an alien individualism on the region's traditional religious order. Most would have preferred to believe with the Pope that Europe must 'breathe with both lungs', and that East and West will be regarded equally as 'keepers of Europeanness'.

Yet this seems increasingly unlikely. After study visits to Brussels in 1997–9, church leaders in Poland, the Czech Republic and Hungary are now formally supporting their countries' admission to the European Union, under formal negotiation since October 1998. But some Catholic bishops are worried that the opening of borders will have a profound impact on social and moral habits. This is hardly surprising. Besides incorporating the *acquis communautaire* – the EU's body of regulations and procedures – and ensuring their laws and institutions meet the criteria set out in the 1950 European Convention, candidate countries must meet stringent inflation, interest-rate, budget deficit and currency goals, at a time when Poland's average earnings are less than a tenth of neighbouring Germany's. In agriculture alone, the country will need drastic, prolonged change.

In a 1998 survey, 84% of Polish priests supported their country's EU accession, with two-thirds voicing confidence that membership would not affect the church's position.[10] But church leaders are determined to ensure their region's Christian culture is properly protected. Four decades ago, they point out, when the first EU prototype institutions were formed, the churches of Spain and Italy were as full as Poland's are today, while the Dutch Church sent as many priests abroad as missionaries. The trend in religious observances and church affiliations has been unmistakably downwards.

To make matters worse, churches were not even mentioned in the 1992 Maastricht Treaty, under which EU member-states agreed to closer political and economic links. A brief statement recognizing the 'status enjoyed by churches and religious associations and communities' was accepted by EU foreign ministers at their 1997 Amsterdam summit, after German theologians had warned of a 'crisis in legitimacy'.[11]. Despite EU assurances that traditions will be preserved, however, many fear that membership will require the acceptance of Western secular models.

The East European Church has no equivalent to the Brussels-based Commission of Episcopal Conferences of Europe (COMECE), drawn from the European Union's fifteen member-states, which has met twice yearly since its foundation in 1980 to monitor EU affairs. It is also hamstrung by a complex web of regional inter-faith relations, particularly between Catholic and Orthodox communities, reflecting the role of religion as a focus for post-Communist loyalties and identities which has no equivalent in the West. This has made it harder for East European Catholics to articulate a common position.

Shifting these anxieties will require time, as well as a readiness to resist stereotypes. In reality, Eastern Europe is not as religious as some church leaders would like to believe. Nor is Western Europe as secular. Although 40% of the Czech Republic's 10.5 million citizens declared themselves Catholics in a late 1999 survey, church sources estimate that no more than one in ten Czechs are even Christians.[12] Meanwhile, professed atheists number as many as 40% in the former East Germany, compared to a European average of 5%.

In Western Europe, the Irish can still rival the Poles as Europe's most religious nation. But only a quarter of Germans practise their faith, twice as many as in France. Although 63% of marriages end in divorce in Sweden, the figure for Italy is 10%, below that of Poland.[13]

Contrasting experiences of the twentieth century have fuelled deep differences of sentiment and perception which will only be neutralized as forms of comprehension and empathy gradually evolve. Only then will Eastern Europe's church find its rightful place within the universal church as co-creator and co-beneficiary of the church's richness.

Notes

1. Delo interview, 18 September 1999.
2. Encyclical *Pacem in terris* (11 April 1963), Nos. 158–9.
3. *Gaudium et spes* (7 December 1965), No. 63; Declaration on Religious Liberty, *Dignitatis Humanae* (7 December 1965), No. 15.
4. 'Pro Memoria Episkopatu Polski of sytuacji Kosciola', in Peter Raina (ed.), *Kosciol w PRL – Dokumenty 1960–1974*, Poznan 1995, 682–7.
5. *Report of the Crimea Conference*, London 1945, 4–5.
6. Encyclical *Laborem exercens* (14 September 1981), No. 8.
7. 'Speech to clergy, religious and committed laity', St Vitus Cathedral, Prague;

Holy See Press Office, 21 April 1990. See also Jonathan Luxmoore and Jolanta Babiuch, *The Vatican and the Red Flag*, London 1999.

8. 'Europa ma racje poszukujac duszy'; *KAI Biuletyn Prasowy*, Warsaw, 14 September 1999.

9. 'Troski i nadzieje', *KAI Biuletyn Prasowy*, 1 October 1999. Polish Church figures from Church Statistics Institute, Warsaw, 1997 and 1999.

10. *Centrum Badan Opinii Spolecznej (CBOS)*, survey *in Rzeczpospolita*, 24 March 1998, and *Polityka*, 28 March 1998.

11. Jonathan Luxmoore, 'The European Union looks East', in *Our Sunday Visitor*, 12 July 1998.

12. *Katolicky tydenik* survey, 5 December 1999.

13. For comparative figures, see Paul M. Zulehner, ed., *Kirchen im Übergang in freiheitliche Gesellschaften, Pastorales Forum*, Vienna 1994; Miklós Tomka and Paul M. Zulehner, *Religion in den Reformländern Ost (Mittel)Europas*, Ostfildern 1999; Miklós Tomka and Paul M. Zulehner, *Religion im gesellschaftlichen Kontext Ost (Mittel)Europas*, Ostfildern 2000; Jonathan Luxmoore and Jolanta Babiuch, 'New Myths for Old', *Journal of Ecumenical Studies*, Vol. 36, Nos. 1–2, 2000.

Encounters Between East and West in the Renewal of Pastoral Work

PAUL M. ZULEHNER

Where they could not destroy the churches, the Communists turned them into museums. In doing so the regimes in the individual countries of Eastern (Central) Europe adopted differing measures. Moreover the time of harsh persecution was followed by a diminution, especially after 1975. Nevertheless assumptions and also measures continued to remain.

The assumptions were as follows. Religion is hostile to Communist progress, serves as an opiate to divert people from changing circumstances, and is therefore something like alcohol to alcoholics. So the dissolution of religion was carried out in the interest of emancipation, now above all social emancipation. However, it was also clear to the consistent Marxists that religion would disappear only along with poverty. The Communists also worked hard to remove the latter.

The measures taken were these. Religion (and with it the churches) was to be removed from society. In this sense the privatization of religion was a decisive measure in the fight over religion. The churches were also deprived of all instruments of their social presence: Caritas, the associations, the schools, the religious orders. For those who still needed religion all that was left was life in the sacral ghettos. Not least the channels of tradition were cut: religious education as part of public religious education, and the socialization of upbringing in general by weakening the role of families and parents in upbringing.

These measures were more or less successful in all Communist societies. The retreat into the sacristy took place as a process of transforming the church and led to both a spiritual strengthening and a spiritual weakening.

I. The change

This was the situation in which the churches of Eastern (Central) Europe experienced the change – which had been brought about in the midst of

societies which were structurally on the way to democratic conditions and
with people who for decades had been shaped as *homo sovieticus*: provided
with social welfare, with a highly privatized life, intent on his own happi-
ness, deeply mistrustful of everyone including friends – and rightly so, as is
shown by the publication of the secret files of the state police forces.

In this situation the church did not have very many basic pastoral options.

A first option can be called nostalgia. It lives by the attempt to pick up
church life where the Communists interrupted its development. That
included the establishment of the old institutions (religious orders, schools),
and thus also the demand for a return of estates and property, in the name of
justice. This first option cost the churches a great deal of effort, but also a
loss of credit in the eyes of the people. For even poor churches (not least after
the successful opinion-making by the Communists) were suspected of being
rich. In addition, the young Reform democracies were in an economically
precarious situation. But pastorally, too, this option failed: most churches
did not have the manpower, or the religious orders the members, to run all
these institutions as in pre-Communist times.

A second option can be called orientation on the West. Just as democracy
and (though hardly a social matter) the market economy entered the post-
Communist countries from the West, so too 'Western' experiences of the
church were to be taken over. The prime example here is East Germany,
where the church (like other social spheres), was in fact incorporated into
Western structures, with church tax, religious instruction in schools and a
structure of associations. In other countries this orientation on the West had
a negative effect. The old hostile stereotype was largely replaced by the new
stereotype of liberalism. Just as some wanted to take over the supposed
strengths of Western churches, others remained trapped in fighting off
Western weaknesses. And because a development back into the pre-
Communist period (option 1) obviously would not work, but 'Westerniza-
tion' was vehemently fought against, such spheres of the church remained
as they were under Communism: privatized, removed from society, and
concentrated on the liturgy and the clergy.

Gradually a third option is developing, which envisages a long haul. In a
first stage it is concerned to assimilate the experiences of the church in the
Communist period. That is also theologically appropriate. It could well be
that God himself has led these areas of the church into this condition, as
Israel was once led into captivity: 'Thus says the Lord of hosts, the God of
Israel, to the whole community of the exiles whom I have led away from
Jerusalem to Babylon' (Isa.29.4). But what is the teaching of this time? What

have these regions of the church – and beyond them all the people of God dispersed in many churches – to learn? And conversely, what do they have to unlearn?

On the initiative of the Pastoral Forum in Vienna (of which Cardinal Dr Franz König, who did so much work to protect the church in Eastern [Central] Europe in the Communist era, is president), men and women from Eastern (Central) Europe who have an academic concern with pastoral theology have met in three symposia to investigate these very questions.

Here there has been a strict methodology which – in the absence of Western pastoral theologians – aims at bringing professionals from the post-Communist countries to a position where they can exchange qualified experiences and ensure that these experiences are also reflected on in a scholarly way. Two great complexes of themes quickly crystallized, and priority over methodology was given to reflection on them. On the one hand there was the question of *Gaudium et spes* (the Pastoral Constitution of the Second Vatican Council). How did the churches in individual countries, each with its own history and cultural traditions, position or not position themselves in the Communist societies, and what does their new position look like in the course of the democratization of these countries? Can they appropriately fulfil the social task of preaching the gospel? On the other hand, from this point questions are asked in the style of *Lumen gentium* (the Vatican II Constitution on the Church) about the self-organization of the church: how can the church organize itself internally in an appropriate way in order to regain its social effectiveness or to reinforce it by reforms?

The proceedings of the symposia have been published – by its own publishing house. They were edited by András Máté-Tóth of Hungary and Pavel Mikluszak of Slovakia and published as the last volume of the publication series of the great Eastern (Central) European research project Aufbruch (New Departures), on the positioning of the churches under Communism and their repositioning in the social transformation. The programmatic title will be: 'Not like Milk and Honey. Towards an East (Central) European Pastoral Theology'.[1]

II. Learning and unlearning

So this third option represents a reactive interplay between learning and unlearning. A series of learning and unlearning themes were identified at the second symposium of East (Central) European pastoral theologians.

From the experiences of the church in the Communist period, among other things the church can learn the valuable things that the church under Communism learned for its action, what it should preserve. Here the key themes are:[2]

1. *In the direction of the 'world': autonomy, a guardian of freedom, critical discussion with the currents of the time, 'a defensive' strategy which holds the church together; an attitude of* diakonia *instead of triumphalistic power;*
2. *In respect of personal faith:* martyria *(witness), solidarity with the believers, among those in office (productive relations with these);*
3. The laity as the subject of pastoral work: new forms of lay organizations, voluntary work, pastoral action with explicit episcopal introduction and regulation (subsidiarity) and without institutional means, small informal groups with an intensive community life, closeness of the community to the bishops;
4. *Development in the sphere of preaching and catechesis: adult catechesis (catchumenate), a deepening of sacramental catechesis, flexibility to take account of different levels in the church, the development of pastoral models, a specific parish catechesis at the parish level, religious courses of a week for children;*
5. *A basic Catholic attitude, a link with the world church or the desire for such a link;*
6. *Ecumenical collaboration.*[3]

Over against this are areas where things need to be unlearned, things which cannot go on as they did under Communism but must be renewed:

1. *An end to ghettoizing, 'out of the niche', acting instead of reacting;*
2. *An end to clerical thinking in terms of power and the infantilization associated with it. A furthering of dialogue within the church and the responsibility of individuals, an end to narrow priestly training;*
3. *A farewell to 'one-man' clerical pastoral work and the limitation of pastoral work to the sacraments. The development of parish and social dimensions for personal believing.*[4]

III. The training of leaders

In addition to the organization of these symposia with the aim of developing a 'Pastoral Theology after the Gulag', the Pastoral Forum has devoted itself to a wider project, namely the training of church leaders. First of all came training with the Czechoslovak and (after the division of the country) with the Czech and Slovak bishops' conferences. The Hungarian bishops also underwent similar training. Theological questions were taboo at these first attempts.

In collaboration with the Society for Personal and Organizational Development, in a second stage two small training groups were set up in order not only to discuss how to develop larger organizations but also how to practise competent leadership. In these groups there was not only the development of competent leadership but also reflection on pastoral theology and supervision. It was important that these groups were formed of leaders not only from post-Communist countries but also from the West European dioceses. Here a declared subsidiary aim alongside the improvement of competence in leadership was that leaders from the two parts of Europe should meet at intervals over two years, exchange experiences and thus learn from one another.

IV. Exchange of experiences among bishops

Such learning from and with one another was initiate at the episcopal level after 1989 by the Council of the European Bishops' Conferences (CCEE).[5]

In 1992 the theme – after the first Synod of Europe called by the Vatican – was 'Living the Gospel in Freedom and Solidarity'.

Another meeting of the bishops took place in 1994, between the two pan-European symposia and after the Synods of Europe called by Rome. At it they exchanged their experiences in Communist times: this material, so far unedited, is awaiting release for publication in the secretariat of the CCEE.

In 1996 the CCE devoted itself to the still pressing theme of 'Religion as a Private Matter', a phenomenon which had been imposed on the churches in the Communist countries and which in the free countries of Europe was proving to be a side-effect of the development of a culture of freedom which was focussed on individuals and their self-guidance. The results of this important symposium are relatively little known. Pastoral guidelines were worked out in which the experiences of the churches in Communism were attuned with those of the churches in the free countries. A kind of European pastoral scheme developed.

I shall document here central passages from this text which is largely unknown in the professional theological world, since I think that it can point the way in relation to the social challenges facing the churches throughout Europe.

The first part of the text contains five basic theological theses.

1. *In the context of freedom it is not only useful but absolutely necessary also to shape encounter with modern men and women in keeping with the nature of God's revelation, in other words, in the form of dialogue.*
2. *Evangelization takes place in dialogue not only with individuals but also with the whole culture.*
3. *Precisely because modern men and women are increasingly often closed to heaven, the church must give them what they lack: a life under the open heaven (Acts 7.55).*
4. *The solidarity which the church needs for survival today will grow particular when the church lives its very own life, namely when it is a 'sacrament of the innermost union with God and the unity of all mankind' (LG 1).*
5. *Men and women of our day expect to be listened to and expect their concerns to be taken seriously. Accordingly, at the level of the tradition of the church official authority must be exercised not only personally and collegially, but above all synodically.*

Then follow basic standpoints and pastoral guidelines for the church's presence in societies and the effect of this on life at home. A culture of freedom and solidarity is called for in the internal architecture of the church. That gives the church the credibility of also being a social force for freedom and solidarity. Here is the section on the involvement of the church in social processes:

Instruments

1. *The 'round table' as an instrument of dialogue: in order to bring the gospel to bear in the midst of social diversity, dialogue must be entered into with representatives of the diverse positions. 'Round table' meetings are well suited to this: at them the churches can ask questions (where do we stand, what solutions are there, what political steps are planned, what are the consequences?), argue, discuss and convince. Solutions, however right they may seem, cannot be forced on people.*

   The round table involves conversation behind closed doors, but also discussion in the media, above all board discussion of drafts of pastoral letters.

   How can individuals (including the bishop) be prepared for taking part in such round-table discussions? Are the churches social academies? How is the laity trained in politics? What contact does the church maintain with the professionals over social concerns?

2. *The church's own institutions: the question in many countries is whether the church should develop its own social institutions (like schools, hospitals, kindergartens, etc.), or whether well-educated laity with church links should work in the public institutions. The question is whether, for example, it is better to train many good teachers than simply to maintain church private schools.*

3. *Presence through the laity: the presence of the church in social life cannot take place simply through those in office (the bishop, the president of the conference of bishops). That applies above all if the church decides not to build up a church counter-society but to help to shape the existing society form within in the power of the gospel. For that it needs trained laity. What are called for are lay organizations capable of action, which are authorized to act for the church in society.*

4. Theology has something to say not just to the church but also to society. Therefore theological institutions are important for the involvement of the church in the development of culture and society. Theology will be able to fulfil its social task all the more easily if it is associated with other university disciplines. Independently of this position of scholarship in scholarly study, an intensive relationship between bishop and theologians is indispensable for the presence of the church in modern cultures. What is called for is the training of theological professionals. They also need working conditions which are as good as possible.

5. Media presence: the church of the world must seek its place in a culture of the image. The culture of the image means television, video and the Internet. Without a qualified presence in this world of the image the church will find it difficult to perform its social task.

6. Are we clearly aware of the particular audiences which we are addressing? Or do we prefer to speak in general terms? Can we make an evaluation of the presence of the church in the media? Are we encouraging laity to intensify the presence of the church in the media, and above that in art and culture?

V. Human investment

One important initiative of many church institutions in the West can best be described as human investment. We want bodies, not buildings, is the motto of the Vienna Pastoral Forum for the advancement of the church in Eastern (Central) Europe, so many men and women have been given the possibility of studying theology in Western faculties not only by this small private association but also with private and church grants. The Pastoral Forum also encourages field studies: thus three Poles in Vienna went to study the excellent religious education done with handicapped children in Catholic and Protestant institutions and to play it back to the Polish church. Many gained doctorates and some even habilitations. This encouragement of theologically well trained people is needed because theology too is impoverished in Communism. There are no resources, books, possibilities of travel; thus for a long time theologians under Communism were cut off from the great European theological dialogue.

Moreover in recent years the Pastoral Forum has succeeded in establishing a chair of Applied Religious Studies at the JATE University in Szeged (Hungary) which for long decades was purely Communist. That too is an important step in the development of the churches. Through believing professionals they can take part in the social process of scholarship. In this way some competition is established, which some Eastern (Central) European churches have neglected either by their own decision or on the instruction of the Vatican Congregation for Education, namely by formally incorporating themselves in the structure of the universities through theological faculties and thus being able to collaborate from within in interdisciplinary research. The future of the sciences, especially the humane sciences, lies with inter–disciplinary work.

Translated by John Bowden

Notes

1. Schwabenverlage, Ostfildern 2000.
2. Actual quotations from the proceedings are printed in italics.
3. *Unterwegs zu einer Pastoraltheologie in nachkommunistischen Ländern. Erstes Symposium von Pastoraltheologinnen und Pastoraltheologen aus nachkommunistischen Landern Europas in Alsópáhok (Ungarn) von 28.9. bis 1.10.1997*, ed. Paul M.Zulehner and András Máté-Tóth, Vienna and Szeged 1998, 73f.
4. Ibid., 75.
5. Here it should not be overlooked that even in Communist times bishops from the West and the East of Europe met at regular intervals at the symposia of the CCEE to exchange information. However, this was not so much a matter of pastoral learning as of church politics and brotherly support of the churches in the persecution.

Contributors

JAN SOKOL was born in Prague in 1936; he is married with three children, a goldsmith and mechanic, and has studied mathematics. Between 1964 and 1990 he was active in developing software. In 1977 he was a signatory of Charta 77, and in 1990–1992 was Vice-President of the Federal Parliament of Czechoslovakia. Since 1993 he has taught philosophy at the Catholic University and in 1998 became Minister of Education in the Czech Republic. His numerous publications include: *Meister Eckhart und die mittelalterliche Mystik* (1993), *Mensch und Welt in der Sicht der Bibel* (1993), *Eine Bibellesung* (1996), *Zeit und Rythmus* (1996), *Eine kleine Philosophie des Menschen* (^{3}1998), *Der Mensch als Person* (2000).

Address: c/o Ceská Krestanská Akademie, Vysehradská 49, CY 12000 Praha 2, Czech Republic.

ALBERT FRANZ was Professor of Philosophy in the Theological Faculty of Trier from 1988 to 1992; since 1993 he has been Professor of Systematic Theology at the Technical University of Dresden. Most recently he has edited *Glaube – Erkenntnis – Freiheit. Herausforderungen der Gnosis in Geschichte und Gegenwart*, Paderborn 1999.

Address: TU Dresden, Philosophische Fakultät, Weberplatz 5–10, D-01217 Dresden, Germany.

ANDRÁS MÁTÉ-TÓTH was born in 1957 in Kalocsa, southern Hungary; he is married and has four children. He studied theology in Szeged, Hungary, and in Vienna, where he gained his doctorate in 1991 and his Habilitation in pastoral theology in 1996. He is founder and director of the chair of religion in the University of Szeged, and co-ordinator of the international research project Aufbruch (New Departures). From 1993–1998 he was chief editor of the Hungarian pastoral theological journal Egyházfórm (Church Forum).

He has many publications in Hungarian on developments in society and the church. Also: *Bulányi und die Bokor-Bewegung. Eine pastoraltheologische Würdigung*, Vienna 1996; *Unterwegs zu einer Pastoraltheologie in den post-sozialistischen Länder* (edited with Paul M. Zulehner), Dokumentations-bände I–III, Szeged and Vienna 1997ff.; *Theologie der Zweiten Welt*, Ostfildern 2000.

Address: H-6701 Szeged, Postfach 777. E-mail: matetoth@rel.u-szeged.hu

MILOSLAV CARDINAL VLK is Archbishop of Prague and President of the Czech Conference of Bishops; he is also President of the Council of European Bishops' Conferences.

JANUSZ MARIANSKI was born in Borowo in 1940. Between 1965 and 1968 he engaged in special studies in the social science in the Faculty of Christian Philosophy of the Catholic University of Lublin. He gained his doctorate in 1972 and his Habilitation in 1979, and since 1984 has been Professor of Moral Sociology at the Faculty of Social Sciences of the Catholic University of Lublin. He is a member of many Polish and international scholarly societies and chief editor of the sociology section of the *Katholische Enzyklopädie*. He is the author of more than 450 articles and 24 books in Polish.

Address: Catholic University, ul. Obroncow Pokoju 11/7, 20–30, Lublin, Poland.

MIKLÓS TOMKA was born in 1941; he studied in Budapest, Leuven and Leiden. He is a member of the editorial board of *Concilium* and Professor of the Sociology of Religion in Szeged, Hungary. He has also been visiting professor in Bamberg, Innsbruck and Salzburg. He is head of the Centre for Philosophy of Religion in the Institute of Philosophy of the Hungarian Academy of Sciences. A co-founder of the Hungarian Pastoral Institute (in 1989), he is also director of the Hungarian Religious Research Centre.

Address: H-1171 Budapest, Várviz u. 4. E-mail: tomka@hcbc.hu

MARKO KERŠEVAN was born in 1942. He is Professor of Sociology and the Sociology of Religion at the Philosophical Faculty of the University of

Ljubljana in Slovenia. He has done research as a Humboldt scholar at the universities of Constance and Tübingen (1972, 1989). His publications are on the Marxist theory of religion, the Protestant theology of Karl Barth, religion in modern society from a sociological perspective and religion and the churches in the (post-)socialist countries; they include: 'Religion and the Marxist Concept of Social Formation', *Social Compass* XXII, 3–4, 1975/3–4; 'Religionssoziologie, Religion, Theologie', in *Science and Faith*, ed. F. Rode and Z. Roter, Ljubljana and Rome 1984; 'Religiosität der Jugend in Slowenien/Jugoslawien' in *Jugend und Religion in Europa*, ed. U. Nembach, Frankfurt am Main 1987; 'Religion und Kirche in der Slowenischen Zivilgesellschaft nach 1990', in *Religiöser Wandel in den postkommunistischen Ländern Ost- und Mitteleuropas*, ed. D. Pollack, I. Borowik and W. Jagodzinsk, Würzburg 1998; and 'Europäer von Morgen – Christen ohne Kirche, Menschen ohne Glaube? Säkularisierung und Pluralismus in Europa', in *Was wird aus der Kirche? 2. Internationaler Kongress Renovabis*, Freising 1998.

Address: University of Ljubljana, Poljanska 54, 1000 Ljubljana, Slovenia.

STANKO GERJOLJ was born in Smolnik, Slovenia in 1955. On leaving school in 1974 he joined the Lazarists and studied theology at the University of Ljubljana. He gained his doctorate in Innsbruck in 1986 with a dissertation on Marxist education as a challenge for catechesis and then studied education and psychology, gaining a doctorate in 1995. After that he was engaged in pastoral work, being director of a private church student hostel between 1994 and 1997. Since 1997 he has been lecturer in education, catechetics and educational psychology in Ljublana. Publications in Germany include: 'Fragen der Identität und Werterziehung in der postkommunistischen Gesellschaft,' in J. Czirják (ed.), *Bedingung der Welt*, Kaposvár 1996, 506–16; 'Biblische Familiendramen aus der erziehungspsychologischer Sicht von Abraham bis Josef aus Ägypten', in J. Czirják, A. Jávorszki and P. Szabóné Gondos, *Letzte Worte*, Budapest 1997, 77–97; 'Perspektiven und Herausforderungen für Gestaltpädagogik in den ehemaligen kommunistisch geprägten Gesellschaften', in H. Neuhold (ed.), *Leben fördern – Beziehung stiften*, Graz 1997, 87–91; *Ideologie und Bildung*, Justus-Liebig-Universität Giessen 1997.

Address: Theological Faculty, University of Ljubljana, Maistrova 2, 1000 Ljubljana, Slovenia.

LÁSZLÓ LUKÁCS was born in 1936. He is a Piarist father, Professor of Dogmatic Theology at the Sapientia Religious College of Theology, Doctor of Theology at the Catholic University of Péter Pázmány and Doctor of Literature at the Eötvös University of Budapest. From 1989–1996 he was president of the European Region of UCIP and since 1998 he has been ecclesiastical advisor to UCIP; in 1989–1993 he was counsellor of the Pontifical Council for the Dialogue with Non-Believers, and since 1995 he has been counsellor of the Pontifical Council for Social Communications.

Address: Information Bureau of the Hungarian Catholic Bishops' Conference, Ferenciek Tere 7–8, 3. Lepscö, ll.em, H-1053 Budapest, Hungary.

VINKO POTOCNIK was born in 1947 in Šoštanj, Slovenia. After studying theology and sociology (in which he gained at doctorate at the Gregoriana in 1980), from 1980 to 1988 he was a student pastor. Between 1982 and 1987 he specialized in pastoral psychology and psychotherapy at the University in Graz, Austria. In 1991 he became lecturer and in 1996 Professor of the Sociology of Religion and Pastoral Psychology in the theological faculty in Ljubljana, appointed to its unit in Maribor. He has collaborated in various research programmes on religion in Slovenia. He has been a collaborator in the international research project 'New Departures' from the beginning. He is co-author of the book *Religion und Kirche in Ost(Mittel)Europa: Ungarn, Litauen, Slowenien* (1999).

Address: Strossmeyerjeva 32a, SLO 2000 Maribor, Slovenia.

JONATHAN LUXMOORE is the Warsaw correspondent of Catholic News Service and Ecumenical News International, and regularly covers church affairs in Eastern and Central Europe for *The Tablet, National Catholic Reporter, Our Sunday Visitor* and other newspapers.

PAUL M. ZUHLEHNER is responsible for the Aufbruch ('New Departures') project based in Vienna.

Address: Kramer-Glöcknerstrasse 36, A-1130 Vienna, Austria.

CONCILIUM

Concilium: Subscription Information

Issues to be published in 2000

February 2000/1: *Evolution and Faith*
edited by Hermann Häring and Christoph Theobald

April 2000/2: *Creating Identity*
edited by Hermann Häring, Maureen Junker-Kenny
and Dietmar Mieth

June 2000/3: *Religion During and After Communism*
edited by Miklós Tomka and Paul M. Zulehner

October 2000/4: *The Bright Side of Faith*
edited by Elsa Tamez and Ellen van Wolde

December 2000/5: *In the Power of Wisdom*
edited by Maria Pilar Aquino and Elisabeth Schüssler
Fiorenza

To receive *Concilium 2000* (five issues) **anywhere in the world**, please copy this
form, complete it in block capitals and send it with your payment to:

SCM Press *(Concilium)* 9–17 St Albans Place London N1 0NX England
Telephone (44) 20 7359 8033 Fax (44) 20 7359 0049

☐ Individual   **£25.00/***US$50.00*   ☐ Institutional   **£35.00/***US$75.00*
Issues are sent by air to the USA; please add £10/US$20 for airmail dispatch to all other countries (out-
side Europe).

☐ I enclose a cheque payable to SCM–Canterbury Press Ltd for £/$ ....

☐ Please charge my MasterCard/Visa   Expires...

......................../...................................../............................../................................

Signature ....

Name/Institution ....

Address ....

....

....

Telephone ....Fax ....

E-mail..